Sweatshops in the Sun

"How long," they say, "how long, O cruel nation,
  Will you stand, to move the world, on a child's heart,—
Stifle down with a mailed heel its palpitation
  And tread onward to your throne amid the mart?"

"The Cry of the Children,"
by Elizabeth Barrett Browning

Sweatshops in the Sun

Child Labor on the Farm

by Ronald B. Taylor

foreword by Carey McWilliams

Beacon Press   Boston

Beacon Press books are published under the auspices
of the Unitarian Universalist Association
Simultaneous publication in Canada by Saunders of Toronto, Ltd.

9 8 7 6 5 4 3 2 1

Library of Congress Cataloging in Publication Data

Taylor, Ronald B.
  Sweatshops in the sun.
  Bibliography: pp. 206–212
  1. Children—Employment—United States.
2. Agricultural laborers—United States. I. Title.
HD6247.A4U57   331.3′83   72–6233
ISBN 0–8070–0516–9

Contents

This book is dedicated to child farm laborers
in the hope that one day soon they may find
there is more to childhood than toil, poverty, and
tears

Foreword

Some aggravated social problems need to be exposed not once, but again and again; they may be twice-told tales, but the second, third, or fourth telling may be more important than the first. Take, for example, the perennial problem of child labor in agriculture. Like the larger problem of migrant farm labor, it has engaged the attention of many journalists, investigators, and social scientists. But it has always been difficult to keep public attention riveted on the problem long enough to get substantial results. There are reasons for this intermittent or lapsed public attention factor. Migrant farm labor is seasonal in character. A wretched situation flares up in this crop or that, in Florida or New Jersey or Yakima, Washington. Briefly, while the situation lasts, whether it be a strike or the death of a child in a labor camp, the local press will publish news stories; there may even be a feature story accompanied by an editorial. Possibly—although not likely—a story may go out on one of the wire services. But the crop is soon harvested, the migrants move on, and the story has "disappeared," so to speak, until the next season. Also to be kept in mind is the fact that the worst abuses in farm labor, and notably in child labor, occur off the main highways and in places that are not routinely covered by the mass media. Still another consideration is that farm labor, by and large, has never been organized, which means that it does not encompass a constituency to which politicians must pay attention and legislatures respond. Historically it has been viewed, when viewed at all, from the outside, by observers, and this, too, makes a difference. Still another fact is that important legislative exposés, and the findings and recommendations of such committees, have often been pushed to one side by some untoward happening or event, such as the outbreak of war. The Industrial Relation Commission hearings were largely forgotten with this country's entrance into World War I. The extraordinarily fine hearings of the La Follette Committee were, in effect, nullified by the attack on Pearl Harbor. The outbreak of the Korean War pushed aside, for the time being, a mounting public concern with "wetbacks." And so it has gone.

Thus Ronald B. Taylor's most readable and thorough investigation of child labor in agriculture updates an issue which has disturbed the American conscience not once but many times. That the problem is still with us hardly requires proof. Something like a fourth of the country's farm workers in 1970 were underage. The existing legislation aimed at prohibiting or regulating employment of minors in agriculture is spotty, full of loopholes, and laxly enforced. For migrant farm workers and their children, working and living conditions are sub-sub-substandard in most parts of the country. Housing is generally wretched. Families are forced to travel great distances, under difficult circumstances, to "follow the crops." They are often swindled or exploited by labor contractors or so-called crew men. The work is seasonal. Wages, by the day or hour or at piece rates, are minimal. (If American agriculture paid wages comparable to those in industry it would add an estimated $3 billion to the costs of agricultural production.) Most farm labor is monotonous drudgery. It is often dangerous and can be—with the new pesticides—extremely hazardous. Health services are inadequate when available. The education of migrant children is far below the norm. Many children of migrants work when they should be in school. The temporary schools set up to accommodate them in some localities are makeshift affairs at best. And worst of all, poverty locks these children into a cycle of poverty from which it is difficult to escape. The parents, in far too many instances, feel that their children must work, so they collaborate with employers in evading the laws. And the laws themselves are inadequate. Historically most labor legislation, state and federal, has contained provisions exempting farm labor.

All this is fairly familiar but it needs—it demands—insistent restatement and updating. *Sweatshops in the Sun* is an excellent summation of the problem on a national scale. Ronald B. Taylor, who has reported on farm labor and farm conditions in California's San Joaquin Valley for some years, is a fine investigative reporter. An admirable quality of this book is that he has interviewed many migrants, young and old—Chicanos, Anglos, and Blacks—in many states, in a wide variety of crops, and he lets them speak for themselves. They are often eloquent, almost invariably vivid, and frequently most perceptive. Taylor wisely lets them tell their own stories, in their own way, and in their own words. The narrative, which moves briskly, is not burdened with too many facts and figures; the reader's attention is kept focused on the people—what they do, how they feel, how they live. Taylor knows farm labor well. He knows, for example, that folklore to the contrary, much farm labor is highly skilled. Migrants habitually follow certain crops—tomatoes, grapes, cotton, strawberries, onions; some specialize in tree or orchard crops—and they become extremely proficient in these particular assignments. A special virtue of Taylor's reporting is that while he views with compassion and listens with sympathy and close attention, he is not sentimental. And he is also fair-minded. He has sought out the employers, the growers, and listened to them; he knows that they too have problems.

It is possible, of course, that mechanization will eventually "solve" the farm labor problem; the number of farm workers has dropped by 1.9 million in the last decade. Even so the federal government continues to subsidize research that will no doubt result in still further mechanization, with increased production and profits for the conglomerates that are now rapidly moving into "agri-biz," taking over, in some instances, from the individual corporate farms about which I wrote in 1939 in *Factories in the Field*. But we have not reached that point yet, by any means. For years to come the residual aspects of "the problem" of child labor in agriculture will be with us and while the reduction in numbers may make it easier to cope with some aspects of the problem, it will also tend to obscure and minimize the major issues involved. Then, too, at some point in time, we may begin to have some misgivings about conglomerate farming and the disappearance of the family-sized farm. We may come to feel that it is important, if only as an interim measure, to keep more people in rural areas engaged in agricultural pursuits. Cesar Chavez and his colleagues are convinced, and with good reason, that it is possible to work out a satisfactory full-time work cycle for farm workers, a pattern of employment that would provide year-round employment at competitive wages, with decent housing and health services, and with schools which the children of farm workers could attend as other children do, on a regular full-term basis. *Sweatshops in the Sun* serves, therefore, an important social purpose; it will stand as a reminder of an acute social problem which is still very much with us and also as a kindly but firm rebuke for the way in which we continue to neglect it.

Carey McWilliams

Preface

As a reporter I have specialized in the subjects of poverty, prejudice, and privation that are the daily life of the rural poor. Over the years I have written thousands of words about farm workers and their families; although the children were sometimes a part of those stories, usually the focus was on the problems faced by the families or by the adult workers.

Before Beacon Press asked that I write this book I was aware of the children working on farms, I knew they lived in the shanty labor camps and rundown farm worker communities and that they labored beside their parents in the fields. They were a small, appealing part of the rural poverty scene.

But gathering information for *Sweatshops in the Sun* was my first real attempt to concentrate on the world of these small workers, who have always been within sight, but who have so long been ignored. Now, as I drive through the countryside, I find myself looking for children at work, and I see them in surprising numbers and wonder why I hadn't focused my attention on them before. As I worked on this book I began to realize that I had seen these children only as an observer conditioned to the fact that child labor on the farm was a common occurrence, in no way out of the ordinary.

In the year that it has taken to put *Sweatshops in the Sun* together I have had the time to reflect upon what I have seen and to fit these findings into the perspective I have formed over the years. While I have been writing about farm labor for only a decade and a half, my first farm worker recollections date to the 1930's. I was a native Californian, a child growing up during the Great Depression in a small San Joaquin Valley farming town.

Those yeoman farmers, who had been blown out of Oklahoma, Arkansas, and Texas by wind and drought, had come up Route 66 to California seeking work on the farm. To us "town kids" they were "Okies" and they had among them "Goddamn Reds" who would overthrow our government and rape our mothers and sisters.

First the Cannery and Agriculture Workers Industrial Union (CAWIU) and then the Congress of Industrial Organizations (CIO) tried to organize the migrant farm workers. The CAWIU cotton strikes of the early 1930's erupted in violence in which workers were shot and killed by vigilante groups. Then the CIO—the words meant "Come In Okie" to us—took up the effort. There was a park across from the school where the workers held rallies and across from the park was the county jail. I can still remember seeing the barred jail windows crowded with arrested workers yelling out to the mobs of their friends outside.

And I remember that one winter—I think it was 1937–38—it rained heavily and the river flooded. The Okies lived in a shantytown out along River Road. Their hovels were built of sheet tin from old Coca Cola billboards, scrap lumber, and cardboard. There was no work, no food, and their shelters were under water.

Strangely, I don't remember any Mexican-American farm workers. They were there. In Arvin and Pixley some of them died in the riots; they suffered just as the Okies suffered, but they were invisible. Among this invisible army of dark-skinned workers was an Arizona boy, not much older than I. His name: Cesar Chavez. The lessons he learned then are the basis for his work, his outlook, his sense of history. It wasn't until I met Chavez thirty years later, that I realized the prejudice that existed in these San Joaquin Valley towns. Chavez told me how he, as a teen-ager, tried to sit in the Anglo section of a theater; the theater manager asked him to move. When Chavez refused, the manager called the police. It was only when I heard this story that I recalled the seating arrangements in the theater where every Saturday we watched Hopalong Cassidy and Tom Mix win the West. We town kids just assumed the Mexicans and Negroes sat up in back in the right-hand corner because they liked to be together.

During World War II—farm workers were off to war or working in defense plants—the farmers needed help and school children heeded the call to colors. At 13 I was picking peaches and then working in a peach-drying shed, tossing 40-pound lug boxes to the cutters for 35 cents an hour. From there we moved into the raisin-grape harvest and I could "cut" 20 trays an hour, at 5 cents a tray. In the late fall they let us out of school to pick cotton—a job I detested.

My view then, and later when I was a student in an agriculture college, was that of a cowboy conservative. I tried to ride bulls and bucking horses in rodeos and firmly believed in John Wayne and the image he represented.

But within this conservatism there was a germ of an idea, a concern for the children of farm workers. Once, in a rural sociology class term paper, I proposed that the children of farm workers be taken away from their parents—during the winter when there was no work—and placed in retraining camps where they would be taught the basic essentials of middle-class living, things like bathing, brushing their teeth, saving their money, learning to work at decent jobs. When they returned home, I reasoned, they would influence their parents.

At Washington State University I combined the lessons of agriculture with journalism and began to write for farm magazines. During my first years as a general assignment newspaper reporter, I free-lanced "how to do it" farm magazine stories designed to help growers improve their operation or save on labor costs by replacing workers with machines.

In 1955 I also began to write about the rural poor. I had

moved back to California to work for the Fresno *Bee* and was shown a community of Black cotton pickers, in Teviston, who lived in incredible poverty. An American Friends Service Committee worker, Bard McAllister, was working with these people, helping them finance and construct a community water system. These families *had no water*. I was shocked. The men and women were being replaced by machines and had no hope of finding other work. During the winter they starved. I really had never seen such conditions before . . . at close hand. The problems of the community of Teviston in 1955 and 1956 turned me onto the subject of rural poverty. From there it was but a short step into the subject of farm labor.

In the late 1950's and early 1960's, the AFL-CIO made another of its efforts to organize farm workers. The Agriculture Workers Organizing Committee (AWOC) opened offices up and down the San Joaquin Valley, held rallies, and conducted a series of strikes in the cherries, plums, and olives. I was sent out to do the stories. Until this time I had never faced the wrath of a group of farmers who were angered by any press coverage that attempted objectivity. If you were not pro-farmer, they treated you as the enemy.

The AWOC pickets obviously wanted press exposure and would talk; the farmers, on the other hand, refused to say anything, kicked reporters off their farms and out of their meetings, and then damned the press for presenting one-sided stories. The AWOC strikes failed and most of the AWOC organizers drifted away, but in Delano there was one, Larry Itliong, who maintained a viable organization among the Filipino table-grape workers. Chavez—who moved to Delano in 1962—began organizing the Mexican-American grape workers. Itliong and the Filipino workers started the grape strike in 1965 and Chavez and his fledgling National Farm Workers Association joined the effort.

From 1962 to 1972 the course of American agriculture was changed; during this decade much of my reporting was an effort to present and interpret the blow-by-blow account of the farm labor unionization efforts. In this effort to report news and attempt to bring understanding of the basic issues, there was little time for any subjects but those that fell within the confines of the controversy; there was too little time to reflect and to refine the issues, to distill out subjects like child labor on the farm.

Sweatshops in the Sun has given me the time and the scope needed to examine the subject of child labor on the farm. It has allowed me to compare California and Florida and Texas, to go to the roots of the migrant and seasonal farm labor structure, and to see how the children fit into the larger picture. It has given me time to expand my viewpoint, given me a chance to meet and to briefly know hundreds of farm workers and their families across the nation.

In this book I have tried to present as complete a picture of child labor on the farm as possible. In the process I hope I have been able to contribute understanding to the complex problems these children, and their parents, face. And I hope in the end I have made the point that the struggle between the worker and the grower is not a contest to determine who is *right* and who is *wrong*; it is a power struggle and for the worker that struggle is for the very existence of his family.

I have purposely changed the farm workers' names in this book to protect their identity. While some of the workers and their families talked candidly without the promise of anonymity, others were apprehensive, even fearful. One woman, although obviously nervous about being seen with me, was determined to talk about the intolerable conditions in the fields and the camps where she and her children worked and lived. When two other workers drove up she nearly panicked. She was afraid they would see the tape recorder on the bench between us and report her to the crew boss who controlled their lives.

Since most of these workers establish job patterns that take them to the same areas and into the same fields year after year, I chose to mask their identities so that I would not interfere with their already precarious employment patterns. At the start of each interview I made it clear that I was not going to identify anyone; my purpose was and is to define a complex problem—child labor on the farm—not jeopardize family incomes.

In some instances I have moved the geographic setting of an interview, in others I have added or subtracted from the number of children in a family, or changed their first names and their ages. At no time have I altered the meaning or intent of their words; I have faithfully tried to duplicate their economic and social environment, I have tried to present their side of the story just as I found it.

If in the process of masking the identity of either an individual or a family I have accidentally duplicated the identity of another individual or family, I apologize. I in no way want to make any farm worker's life more difficult; whether that worker is five or fifty years old he or she already suffers far too great a burden.

Ronald B. Taylor

Acknowledgments

How do you acknowledge the contributions of so many who have given of their time, who have contributed their knowledge, who have shared their experiences? In the beginning there were poverty lawyers, union organizers, and social workers all across the country who, on the strength of a phone call or the mention of a mutual friend, would take time out to put me in touch with the problems of child labor, or to help me meet those who were familiar with a geographic area and could act as my guide. There are those Black and Chicano farm workers who took me into the world they know so well and acted as my guide, my sponsor, my interpreter, and in the end talked freely of their own lives so that I might better understand. Without their assistance, without the help of the U.S. Senate Subcommittee on Migratory Labor—and subcommittee counsel Boren Chertkev—this book would not have been possible. Then there are those friends like Harry Bernstein of the Los Angeles *Times* and Deane Wylie of the Fresno *Bee* who took the time to read my work in the rough and make suggestions; there is Mary Zaninovich, who typed my manuscript, and Gene Rose, who worked through my collection of negatives and printed the pictures. For a year my wife Dorothy and our three children have had to live with this project; they have read copy, typed, shuffled papers, and mostly put up with my preoccupation with the work. My employers, the McClatchy Newspapers, and my editors at the Fresno *Bee* allowed me time to work on the project.

I wish to acknowledge Carey McWilliams, the editor of *The Nation*, whose writing has inspired me and whose publication of my pieces on farm labor brought me to the attention of Beacon Press editor Ray Bentley, who suggested I write *Sweatshops in the Sun*.

Saturday's children work hard in the chili pepper,
toting 45-pound sacks, they kneel in the vine rows,
filling their hampers or picking pans and carry these
to the checker's stand. In the apples they scurry
like squirrels, picking the fruit off the ground; in the

*cotton, they work with long-handled hoes beside their
parents; in the berries and grapes they do an adult's
work, even the smallest have their own picking buckets.
Often their labor is supplemental, a part of a total
family effort to survive.*

*Home is often a labor-camp shack, the kitchen a tiny,
grease-spattered stove in the corner of the room that
also serves as the eating and sleeping area. There is
no room for privacy, no place to call your own. As I
have wandered the back-country roads writing the story
of farm labor, I have carried a camera, to illustrate*

*my work. Most of these photographs have appeared
alongside my articles in the* Fresno Bee; *some were taken
in New Jersey and Florida and California especially
for this book. They span the years from 1955 to 1972.
During that time little has changed to improve the
farm worker's living and working conditions.*

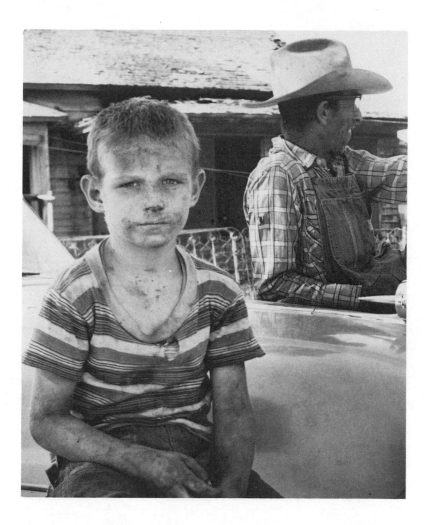

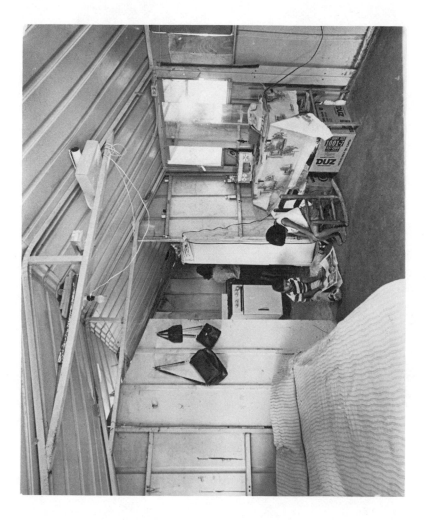

Sweatshops in the Sun

1

"The real problem in America is not child labor, but child idleness. You cannot convince me that it hurts a child either physically or morally to make him work. Where one child, in my experience, has been injured from work, ten thousand have gone to the devil because of lack of occupation."[1]
—*Senator Charles S. Thomas*

The Myths

The judge of a small justice court in rural California fined an employer $33 for allowing an 8-year-old boy to drive a tractor.

The boy's job was to pull a trailer loaded with bins slowly along beside a mechanical tomato harvester. As the machines moved through the field, the boy had to position the bins to catch the fruit pouring off a conveyor belt that projected from the side of the harvester.

The boy was so small he could not reach the tractor clutch or brake pedals. When he wanted to stop, or to shift gears, he had to slip off the seat, then step on the appropriate pedal. The judge agreed the job was dangerous.

Asked why the fine was so small, he responded: "Maybe it was because I was driving a tractor when I was 8 years old. I have a strong belief that 90 percent of our delinquency is caused by the fact that the state has legislated children out of jobs."

The state and federal governments have legislated against child labor, to a limited extent. These laws were passed—after a long, bitter struggle—to prevent the exploitation of children in the mines, in the factories, and in textile mills, and later they were amended to safeguard children from the dangers of mechanized farm work. I don't think the judge wants to see children exploited, nor do I think he was arguing for 8-year-old or 10-year-old tractor drivers. His words had an obvious, deeper meaning to him; he was expressing the commonly held beliefs that labor is virtue and that labor on the farm is the essence of American virtue.

Within the structure of this mythology the farm has been made the basic building block in American culture, the farmer, the chief architect of the American character. What better place for a child to learn the lessons of toil than in the open fields and vineyards first plowed and planted by westering pioneers?

Western man cleared the wilderness, plowed the virgin soil, took a woman to wife; together they created a work force in their own image—the boys to split the rails and harvest the crops, the girls to cook and sew and card and churn. The children drove the cows from the fields, chopped the kindling, and slopped the hogs, and after the chores were done, likely they walked some miles to school where they read in *McGuffey's Reader*: "I doubt if any boy ever amounted to anything in the world, or was much use as a man who did not enjoy the advantages of a liberal education in the way of chores."

The family worked together, generation after generation, sinking their roots into the land, creating a way of life, a culture that had specific social and geographic boundaries. They—the family of the farmer—belonged to the land and the land to them. The size of their venture was limited only by the size of the family, its combined skills, its tenacity, and its willingness to gamble. Hard work became its own reward.

The farmer yoked the oxen, harnessed the power of the horse, and the great midcontinent plains were turned into fields of corn and wheat. Each fall strong men gathered at the county seat to test their newfound powers, to display their skills with plow and seed.

By adding fertilizer and irrigation and mechanization and something the new agriculture schools called "management," they harvested larger crops and displayed the product of their increased skills at the county fair. With the profits of the year, the most successful expanded, purchasing the land of their less efficient neighbors. These successful farmers became proof of the myths.

The mythology that has grown up around the family farm has its roots in the common ideals and emotions that run deep through our culture. We are an agrarian people in transit; we yearn for the idyllic life. It would be nice to be a child again, to milk the cows and slop the hogs and chop the wood and walk to a one-room schoolhouse.

Each weekend millions flee the cities; they head for the wild lands, the open spaces in the mountains, the desert, or the seashore. Never mind that they bring the urban blight with them, that they could not survive without internal combustion engines, space-age electronics, and their aluminum and wood mobile shelters. They are returning to the land, to "nature," to the soil.

There are values to be found within the mythology of the family farm. In exchange for their labor, the land returned to the family food and fiber and a sense of accomplishment. For the sons and daughters there was the closeness of working together with their parents, a sense of identity that linked them with the family land and the surrounding community.

But there are also harsh truths to be discovered beneath the cloak of romantic myth so carefully draped over the family farm. One of these discoveries is that agriculture has always depended upon a supply of cheap labor.

To the family farmer, the labor of his children was essential. Henry Ward Beecher's "A Farm Creed" gave this perspective:

"We believe in good fences, good barns, good farmhouses, good stock, good orchards and children enough to gather the fruit."

As the successful farm grew, an additional source of cheap labor was required. Itinerant, landless men were recruited for the harvest, and another myth was created: the hired harvest hands were a gypsy lot, happy-go-lucky bindlestiffs who worked and drank and whored and drifted through life, never caring a snap for the comforts of home and hearth.

While some could perform prodigious feats of labor, these hoboes were an unreliable lot; they never saved their money, nor settled in for that long, hard pull needed to make something of themselves. All these men needed was a hayloft to sleep in, a horse trough for bathing, a pit privy out back. When they got a few dollars they just headed for town, or the nearest freight train out.

Out West, where adventuresome speculators created large land baronies by manipulating Mexican land grants and United States land law, the great farming empires filled their need for cheap labor by importing Chinese, Mexicans, Filipinos and Dust-Bowl refugees. These workers were not men in the full standing of the word; they were called coolies, peons, boys, or Okies.

As each ethnic group was imported it was touted as better suited for stoop labor than "local" workers. But such praises lasted only as long as the group of workers remained docile. When unrest was detected, when workers showed any sign they were willing to organize, willing to strike for higher wages, they were castigated, intimidated, and finally branded as lazy, trouble-making people who were unsuited for the work.

In the South, the mythology of the family farm was warped to fit the grotesque truth of Black slavery. The legacy of slavery can be seen all over the South. Today the slaves are rented. When the work is over, they are spurned, rejected, told to fend for themselves. In 1970 one Southern farmer expressed his feelings for Black farm workers this way: "You get down to their level, and they have no respect for you. I mean if you want to be down and act like a Negro and be dirty and what not, they are not going to respect you."

The mythology covers another source of cheap labor: children. Each year untold thousands of boys and girls are employed legally and illegally to harvest the nation's crops. The American Friends Service Committee reported: "The use of children as industrial laborers was outlawed under the Fair Labor Standards Act of 1938, yet in 1970 one-fourth of the farm wage workers in the United States are under 16 years old."[2]

The AFSC and various governmental agencies estimate 800,000 children work on farms. This number is a guess and almost certainly does not include thousands of children who work beside their parents, picking into the parental baskets or running and fetching so their parents are free to work faster.

After sending investigators into five states, the AFSC reported: "The child labor scene in the 1970's is reminiscent of the sweatshop scene in 1938."

Such statements brought an angry response from rural America. Letters and editorials denounced the AFSC findings. An Indiana poultryman wrote: "We cannot believe the AFSC would recommend a law to take away the great privilege of work from the few children who still can have it. You should know that work is the greatest thing in the world for children, especially work on the farm . . . six years is none too soon to start work on the farm . . . ."

A southern New Jersey farm wife: "I would rather see a youngster work and learn the ethics of earning money than add our rural youth to the masses of aimless, drifting unemployed urban welfare recipients . . . ."

Small-town newspaper editors were incensed. One wrote: "The AFSC is barking up the wrong bean bush . . . besides having the comradeship of other youths in the platoon, young pickers learn the value of a dollar and the joy of recreation earned; they gain a self-respect deep in the inner person because of having contributed to the world's needs; they help save the strawberries and the beans for canning; and they have earned their own spending money for the summer and next year . . . ."[3]

Such writings are romantic. The authors imply child labor on the farm is being done by the sons and daughters of the farmer and by the urban and suburban youngsters who want to earn pocket money and who would otherwise be unoccupied and into mischief. It is true some of the farm work force is made up of such children, but those who protested the AFSC report were confusing children's work with child labor.

The great majority of children working on farms do so because they must if their families are to survive. There is a terrible difference between doing the chores or earning some pocket money and having to work so your mother and father and brothers and sisters can eat, can afford a place to live and a few clothes to wear. That difference is the difference between children's work and child labor.

The key to understanding farm labor is not found in romance or in mythology, but in economics. The slave, the imported coolie, the child who must help harvest the crops—all have one thing in common. They are cheap labor. The dollar and economic sense of this becomes apparent when a comparison of industrial and agricultural wages is made: If farmers paid industrial wages it would increase their yearly labor costs by $3 billion.[4]

This is a subsidy granted by specific legislative actions. Over the years state and federal legislators have listened to the myths and to the economic woes recited by the voices of agriculture, and have excluded farm workers from protective regulatory labor laws and social reforms.

Farm wages are low because in 1935 agriculture was excluded from the National Labor Relations Act that guaranteed the workers' rights to organize, to strike, and to bargain from their collective, unfettered strength.

Farm wages are low because federal and state minimum wage guarantees to farm labor are so tenuous they are not effective. In 1969 the federal minimum wage for agriculture was upped to $1.30 an hour but it covers only those workers on larger farms. And the law is riddled with exemptions including one that allows farmers to pay migrant children under 16 the prevailing piece rate as long as that scale is being paid to everyone else in the field.

The Fair Labor Standards Act (FLSA) of 1938 made it illegal to employ children under 16 years of age while school was in session and it prevented children from working at specific hazardous jobs. The price the farm-block politicians exacted for passage of the bill was the exclusion of agriculture. Urban pressures were not great enough to overcome this opposition until 1966.

How many children work in agriculture? Mrs. Dale Kloak, chief of the Child Labor Branch, Wage and Hour Division, U.S. Department of Labor, said, "We don't have any detailed figures. It is estimated at 800,000. I think there is no doubt that this is an area in which there is the greatest exploitation of children.

"In a country like this, it would seem we wouldn't have to depend upon the labor of youngsters to keep the families together. This is the kind of thing that went out way back in the 1800's." In rather apologetic terms she added, "We cannot force these children to go to school, but we can keep them from working. We try very hard. I think our staff is devoted to enforcement of the law, but there simply is a limit to what they can do."

In 1967 a small staff of federal investigators found 7,076 children working illegally on 2,300 farms. As the urban liberals who had forced legislators to include child labor on the farm under protection of the FLSA turned to other causes, so did the investigators. Where they had checked 3,500 farms in 1967, they were inspecting only 862 in 1970. On 498 of these farms they found 1,472 children at work during school hours; 61 percent were 14 years old or younger.

The problem with these statistics is that they result from a system that is highly selective. Because they must police all employers covered by the FLSA, the investigators have little time for agriculture. Each fall, as schools open, wage and hour investigators work the farm fields. Most of the violations are found in the vegetables, primarily in tomatoes in Ohio.

If the tomatoes in Ohio ripened earlier and could be harvested before school was in session, there would be no federal violation; if the California raisin grapes matured a week or two late and federal investigators looked into the vineyards, the statistics would soar; if Maine schools were not recessed during the fall potato harvest, there would be several thousand more violations.

The federal child labor laws are weak. Most of the states' are no tougher. But there are exceptions. In California and New Jersey, children 12 years old and older can work on farms when school is not in session, but they must have work permits to do so. In all, 11 states, Puerto Rico, and the District of Columbia specifically provide a minimum age for employment of children in agriculture when school is not in session. Another nine states regulate age only during school hours.

Indiana law says no minor under the age of 14 shall be employed or permitted to work in any gainful occupation other than farm labor. By various semantic devices, Oregon, Michigan, and Washington state legislators similarly exempted agriculture from their child labor laws; in Maine no child under 15 is permitted to work while school is in session unless he is employed by or with or is under the supervision of his parents.

Most states that have child labor laws also have special exemptions for poverty or need; in Florida the law permits minors of 12 years and over to be employed if legally excused from school because of poverty; California makes the same exception for 14-year-olds if they have completed the eighth grade.

For the families that follow the crops the law has no consistency. The children work until they are chased out of the fields, they learn to run and hide if a stranger approaches, they memorize birth dates that make them old enough to work legally. Where there are child labor laws, the enforcement is spotty.

For these families the schools are at best a babysitting service for the younger children. Education is important, but it must come after the family is fed and housed and clothed and enough has been put by to see them through weeks of unemployment. The children go to school when there is no work, or when forced to do so by the law.

As a result nine out of ten migrant children cannot keep up with their school work; most of them fall behind and must repeat a grade every two or three years. An analysis of those children found working illegally showed the educational gap widens as the youngsters grow older and are more able to work. By the time they are 13 or 14 they are full-fledged workers.[5]

Despite the evidence of educational deprivation, the school systems in too many farming areas serve the needs of agriculture first. In Oregon's Willamette and Tualatin Valleys state manpower officials routinely go into the schools to recruit farm labor and the teachers help them inform from 25,000 to 30,000 children aged 8 to 15 of job opportunities in the summer harvest.[6] In Aroostook County, Maine, schools are recessed in the late fall so thousands of school-age children can work in the potato harvest.[7]

In Texas regular schools start in the early fall, two months before thousands of migrant families return home to the Rio Grande Valley. Using federal funds, educators have developed special migrant schools that start in November. The classes run from 8 a.m. to 5 p.m. in an effort to cram a full school year into the migrant child's head before he or she must take off again in the spring.

In Louisiana a federally supported special education program allowed children to work beside their parents from early morning until noon, then they caught a bus and attended classes until 6 p.m. Local school authorities said the migrant parents were really the cause of this program because if the children were not allowed to work, the parents would leave. One official rationalized: "The youngsters are an economic asset to their parents and if they were forced to leave for school at 8 a.m. daddy's little helpers would just have to pick and not go to school at all."[8]

In California, 14-year-old Joaquin was driving a tractor, pulling a trailer loaded with bins beside a tomato-harvesting machine. On Sunday, September 26, 1971, he suffered disabling back injuries. Details of the accident are sketchy, but apparently a conveyor chute, or spout, that carries the fruit from the harvester to the bins hit him in the back, knocking him from the tractor. The grower is said to have paid the initial medical expenses, and the follow-up treatment was done through a county health clinic operated in the camp where the family lived.

The boy missed two weeks of school. The camp manager said, "He was pretty sick all the way through. He was having trouble walking and was still having a bad time when they [the family] went back to Mexico."

The law is clear; Joaquin drove the tractor illegally. The school, the county housing authority, the county health clinic staff, the doctors who treated the boy all knew about the accident, yet no formal action was taken until after the family left the country. Why? Because the parents asked that nothing be done.

When they came up from Mexico in April, an uncle who was also a ranch foreman put them to work. It was he who assigned Joaquin to the tractor. With only five weeks of the season left after the accident, the family wanted to earn money, not ''make trouble.''

Such a case points out the complex web of social, economic, and governmental circumstances that trap children in a system that deprives them of their health, their education, their welfare. This is child labor.

Over and over again farmers ask: ''What does it hurt for a kid to pick a few beans or a few tomatoes?'' The question is intended to preserve the farmers' right to exploit children. In more elaborate terms, the same question is raised by the voice of American agriculture in the halls of Congress to protect this special privilege.

Matt Triggs of the American Farm Bureau put it this way: ''If these kids want to go out and work, they do work. They earn something, earn self-respect and self-reliance. This is the important part of their education. Do we jeopardize this valid, desirable social objective by legislation to flatly prohibit employment of young workers?''

It was afternoon and Triggs and I were standing outside a U.S. Senate hearing room in the nation's capital. He was about to testify against a proposal to extend and increase minimum wage proposals for farm workers.

Earlier that day he had testified against a House bill that would have prohibited the employment of children under 14 years of age. At both hearings the American Friends Service Committee supported the legislation by presenting evidence gathered during their 1970 survey of child labor on the farms.

I asked Triggs about the AFSC report. He said: ''As is often true in reports in this subject area, you can go out and find isolated instances of particular situations and then try to generalize that this is typical, and it isn't. This is not a factual, objective procedure. There is no factual data in this connection, with respect to employment of anybody under 14. So that all anyone can do is express their understanding of the situation and their observations. How many people under 14 are working in agriculture? I don't know. In terms of man days of work, this is a completely inconsequential factor. Farmers simply don't employ people under 14 anymore for a lot of reasons.''

Whether or not farmers ''employ people under 14 anymore'' may be open to technical argument, but there can be no doubt that children under 14 work on farms. Child labor is used extensively in specific crops and in specific areas. In the shade tobacco fields on the East Coast the federal labor department investigators found that children between 7 and 15 years of age were working under the cheesecloth canopies shading the crop.

They reported: ''The space between the rows is too narrow for a mule and too cramped for an adult and the canopy cuts off what little air is circulating, causing intolerable working conditions. One large producer was found illegally employing 28 youngsters during school hours . . . .''

In California the federal investigators found 82 school-age children working on 25 farms producing raisins, figs, or tomatoes. A state labor law investigator estimated 30 percent of the 35,000 workers in the raisin-grape harvest were under 12 years old and therefore were working illegally.

Many of these children are from the cities and they commute daily to the farm with their parents. They ride to work in old school buses belonging to labor contractors who pick up crews in predawn, street-corner shapeups. In Philadelphia half of the day-haul crews being bused into the southern New Jersey berry and tomato fields are under 20. Most are Puerto Ricans or Blacks from the ghettos, 10 to 15 percent are under 12 years old.

Whether day-hauling out of a ghetto or migrating with the crops, the children travel with their parents. Black families in the East Coast migrant stream usually move with a crew leader who furnishes transportation, food, and housing and finds the crew work. The crew is an unrelated mixture of single men, winos, and families. Too often the crew leaders are unscrupulous employers who openly exploit both the workers and the growers.

While some Anglo migrants travel with crew leaders, most move as independents, as "freewheelers." The Anglo families may move in loose affiliation with other families, but they are not tied to any large grouping. The Spanish-speaking migrants coming up out of Mexico and the southwestern United States, on the other hand, travel in extended family groups of 20 or 30 men, women, and children.

These Mexican and Mexican-American families are the backbone of the nation's farm labor force. They are everywhere, traveling in their own pickups and autos, moving by caravan from one state to the next. Each of these families is a crew and within such crews there is a crew leader, a patriarch who establishes and maintains contacts with the growers along the family's route.

In all of these groups the children are part of the work force; their labor is vital to the family income. A child of 5 or 6 is allowed to play most of the time, but they are also asked to fetch and carry, to get a water bottle or a lunch pail. Their work education has begun. The 9- and 10-year-olds supervise the younger children and keep their parents supplied with empty picking containers. They also pick some and help in other ways.

While these children may not be worth a day's wages to the grower, they free the parents from the small, time-consuming tasks that slow the work down. Because most of these families work on a piece-rate system, their daily pay depends upon the total number of baskets or boxes picked. By the time the youngsters are 14 or 15 they are considered adult workers and the smaller children are expected to help them too.

The families tend to specialize in crops. They set up routines of travel and work. Some stay with row crops, never working the vines or the fruit trees; some specialize in a single crop, following the harvest through 4 or 5 states; others go to a specific region and work both the trees and the row crops. The goal is to get as many days of peak harvest work as possible.

The work is tiring. To bend and stoop and kneel and crawl for 8 hours, pushing and tugging a basket that weighs up to 40 pounds when filled is back-breaking. To have to carry that basket to the end of the long row, or across the field to a grader or check stand, strains the muscles. This is dulling, mind-numbing work.

A strong, tall Black woman explained why when she worked she wore a large straw hat and under it a scarf that covered all of her face except for her eyes and nose: "It shades you if the sun's out and if it's rainin' it helps keep the water off. Mostly it protects you. Then there's that green, sticky stuff they spray on the vines to kill the bugs, it gets all over you if you ain't covered up."

At work she also wears a long-sleeved shirt and two pairs of men's pants. Most of the crews dress in similar fashion for protection from the elements, the pesticides, and the abrasive contact with the ground when they crawl on their knees.

Crops like strawberries and tomatoes hug the ground. Workers couldn't possibly bend all day, so they work on their knees, but after a while that becomes so painful they sit and scrunch along, then stand and bend, then kneel again, trying to escape the pain and all the while trying to keep a steady picking pace.

"After the day's done, it is all you can do to straighten up, collect your pay, and walk on out of there. Sometimes you hurt so bad you can't fix supper or clean up or anything. You just shuck your clothes and fall on the bed." The Black woman sat outside her tiny labor-camp cabin, cleaning a huge fish; it was late fall, hurricanes had drenched the southern New Jersey coast and the heavy clouds still hung low over the land. It was hot and humid and great black flies, attracted by the smell of the fish, swarmed around us.

Mrs. Rachel Jones was a self-reliant woman in her middle forties. There once had been beauty in her face, but time and circumstance had not been kind. All season she and her three children had worked, in the pickles, tomatoes, and strawberries— ''We was gettin' 10 cents a quart and could make but $3 a day because they only let you work mornin's.''

Now the season was over, the camps were being closed, and the migrants were headed south, back to Florida. It had been a bad year for most. For Mrs. Jones it was a financial disaster. She had spent the previous winter in Florida in a camp belonging to this crew leader. She does not like the migrant stream and wants very much to break out of it, but she was broke.

''I had to come back up this year. There wasn't no choice, 'cause there wasn't nothin' to do in Florida. So I said to myself, 'One more time, I'll try it one more time.' But I had to borrow $110 to get by until we got up here and got to workin'.

''Now the season's gone and I ain't no more than paid The Man [crew leader] what I owed him. It ain't right that you should work so hard an' not have nothin' when you finished.''

There were 60 people in the crew. The families were housed in a long wooden building that had been cut up into one-room apartments. Each had two beds. The crew leader let families cook at a portable kitchen he had rigged on the back of a truck. The single men lived in a barracks nearby and ate in a central dining hall run by the crew leader.

Near the end of the season some of the men had gotten into a fight during a crap game and before it was over several ''got some stitches to sew up where they was cut.'' Later someone set fire to the apartment building in retribution. Several families, including Mrs. Jones, lost all of their belongings.

She had moved out of the camp, and now she and the three children were living in one 7-by-15-foot room in a cement block structure. They shared the use of a 20-by-20-foot kitchen with three other families. Two wooden privies sat out back.

As she cleaned the fish and talked, she emphasized her points by waving a big butcher knife, "Children don't have no business on the season. It is not a place for kids. Why? For the simple reason a lot of people drink wine. They raise sand [cause trouble]. Anything come up, they say it. They don't have no respect for nothin'. They don't have no respect for a dog or a cat or nothin'. It ain't no place for a chile . . . ."

Do the children in the camp work?

"Yes sir. All of 'em that isn't in the day care center [for infants and toddlers] is out there in the fields. I don' know if they make 'em work or not, but they all work. If they don't help out, they [families] can't survive, because to tell you the truth, there ain't that much [work] to do."

Do her children, who are 11, 12, and 13, work?

"The first year we come up, no. They didn't. But this year, I have to have 'em help me."

The pay for farm labor is so low even the U.S. Department of Agriculture must admit: "Poverty, as reflected by family income, is widespread among the nation's hired farm workers, both migratory and nonmigratory. Approximately half the migratory workers lived in families whose income fell below $3,000."[9]

According to the USDA there are 2.5 million farm laborers. These figures include anyone who has worked on a farm during the previous year; school children, housewives, migrants, local seasonal laborers, alcoholics gathered up off skid rows by labor contractors. Three hundred thousand are full-time farm workers who earn $3,400 a year, another 300,000 are workers whose earnings come "primarily" from farm labor. Half of the 2.5 million work 137 days and earn about $1,500 a year.[10]

The problem with such figures is that they are nothing more than guesses. They are gathered by state and federal field men and then compiled by USDA statisticians in Washington, D.C. For example, California has long been considered a reliable source of statistical information. The state's Rural Manpower

Division keeps volumes of statistics on cropping patterns, employment patterns, and farm labor needs.

RMD Deputy Director William Tolbert explained the system from which the employment and wage statistics emerge: "We know the man hours per acre that are needed for any crop, and then we simply multiply the number of acres. We inspect the fields to see how the crop is maturing, and how heavy it will be, then we assign the amount of labor we think it will need."

The California RMD offices are a part of a national network of state-operated, federally funded, farm labor placement services. This $23-million program—established by Congress in 1933 to aid the workers, not the farmers—is coordinated and regulated by the federal Rural Manpower Services, a branch of the Labor Department.

Lawyers representing migrant farm workers have attacked the Rural Manpower Services across the nation. The legal complaints and lawsuits contend the RMD offers grower-dominated services that exploit farm workers by referring them to crew leaders and farmers who violate child labor laws, minimum wage laws, social security laws, housing codes, health and sanitation codes.

These complaints, filed with Labor Secretary James D. Hodgson, forced a 10-month, 18-state study of the allegations. The special Labor Department review team supported the case against RMD. In the area of child labor the special investigators found rural manpower offices recruited families and sent them to farms where even the minimum living and working conditions required by law were violated.

In Ohio, where tomato growers have been in flagrant violation of child labor laws, the farmers would request family workers through the local RMD office. The Ohio RMD staff would place orders with rural manpower offices in Texas or Florida. These orders would contain such statements as "Employer will pay $16.50 per worker for transportation expense for all workers over 14 years old who stay until completion of the harvest.''

Ohio schools start in mid-September. The tomato harvest does not end until mid-October. To collect the transportation allowance the migrant family would have to keep their 14- and 15-year-old children out of school, a violation of the Fair Labor Standards Act that requires all youngsters under 16 to be in school.

Some of the tomato growers also offer a 2-cent a hamper "bonus" if the families stay the full season. If a worker—say a 14- or 15-year-old—quits, he or she loses the bonus. This can mean the loss of several hundred dollars in income to the family.

In California families work in the figs, tomatoes, apples, and grapes—the list of crops is long. And where families work, children work. I asked Tolbert if California growers were illegally using child labor.

"It's hard to say."

Has California RMD done any child labor studies?

"No, we haven't. We have very little way of doing it."

Does California RMD make any farm checks to see if there are children under 12 working?

"On children, we have no authority whatsoever, because we do not refer them [children] to jobs."

Technically, Tolbert is right. RMD does not refer children, it refers families to jobs. If the families allow the children to work, that is some other agency's worry. RMD has no enforcement authority.

Three 10-year-old boys sat at the cafeteria table, across from me. It was late summer, and they were attending special classes for migrant children. We four were alone in the cavernous multipurpose room in a rural California elementary school; the hardwood floor had basketball court markings, the rows of long tables were set for lunch, and back off to the side of the stage, the cooks and helpers were clattering pots and pans. Two of the boys were from Texas and came to California regularly in the early spring. They would remain until late fall, then return to the Rio Grande Valley. The third boy was from the barrio in East Los Angeles and each summer he also traveled, working with his mother and sisters in the crops while his father remained behind at his steady job.

All spoke English well; they were bright, happy, and eager to talk to the big Anglo stranger, once they got over their initial shyness. Obviously they liked the school and were comfortable in its surroundings.

Jorge worked the apricots in Salinas and proudly announced, "I have my own plastic bucket, a red one." He was the city boy, small, thin-faced, quick with his movements and his words.

Tino told me he had picked tomatoes for the fresh fruit market and added, "I hated it. All I could make was $1 for all day." The job is a selective one, the picker must know by the pink or red coloring if the fruit is ready.

Carlos was the professional of the trio. He had driven tractors, worked a half-dozen crops, and was leaving shortly for the raisin-grape harvest in Madera County.

The idea of leaving before school was out—even a summer migrant school—no longer had any emotional impact. Carlos had left so many schools he could not remember them all. He talked candidly, seriously, about how he spread the "tablas" (trays) one after another down the long rows.

He warned, "If you are not careful, the edges of the paper tablas cut your fingers, almost like a knife." He held his fingers up to show where he had suffered such cuts. When he had the trays spread, he returned to where his father or mother were cutting the grape bunches and putting them into the big wash pans. It was Carlos' job to dump the pans and spread the fruit on the tablas.

Later I visited Carlos' parents in a labor camp. Without telling them what their son had told me, I asked if their children worked.

They staunchly denied that the 10-year-old, or any of their other younger children, worked. It is possible Carlos was stretching the truth, but I don't think so. He spoke as a worker. He was more serious than the other two boys I had talked to, there was less of the child in him. I think his parents lied because they were talking to a stranger, and it is best to say you comply with the law.

I interviewed a fourth child in that school, a haunting girl of 12. Maria, although she had gone to school both in Texas and California off and on for six years, spoke no English. We talked through an interpreter. She was a pretty child. She wore her hair pulled back, so that it was out of the way. She obviously understood her allotted role in a large family structure and I don't think it has occurred to her to question the life assignment. Because her grandmother was dead, her primary job was caring for her grandfather. Sometimes they traveled alone, sometimes with the family. Maria goes to school when there is no work. In this family, the 14-year-old daughter works full time and Maria's next youngest brother, 10-year-old José, works when school is not in session.

Maria invited me to visit her parents in a county-operated, state-owned, federally financed labor camp. There are 10 in the family, 3 adults and 7 children. Because the cabins are so small, and late afternoon so hot, we sat outside, in the shade of the small, box-like buildings. An old, badly rusted evaporative cooler hung in one window, its squirrel cage-like fan noisily pumping damp air inside.

Maria's parents had just come from work. They had been picking peaches, and they offered me a paper sack filled with the fruit. Each year the family migrates from the Rio Grande Valley to California and returns to Texas by early December. They are buying a small home in a colonia near San Juan; to make the payments, to pay the rent while they are on the road, to buy food and clothing and meet medical needs, it requires as many working hands as possible.

The father explained 10-year-old José could earn $2 or $3 a day by himself. He was a good worker. The boy puffed up in pride as his father talked. But, the father explained, they had lost work that summer because a foreman had insisted José couldn't legally be in the field.

"He threatened us with a lawyer, with a $500 fine, so we didn't go back to work for that man," the father said.

Not all farmers employ children or allow families to work their children in the fields. Most are decent men who oppose the exploitation of children, who work hard themselves and face grave economic crises as their costs spiral upward.

Yet these men still argue the myths of the family farm and the need for children to work. They deny the pay scale is low by citing cases of families who earn thousands of dollars in a few weeks of harvest. While their arguments are factually stated, they grossly exaggerate the picture of yearly earnings. When payroll accounts show José Gonzales earns $100 a day, the accounting does not reveal that it took 8 or 10 pairs of hands to earn that amount. The records don't show the family only works a few weeks at $100 a day, that many days their labor earns only $30 or $40, that the family must sometimes go days or weeks without work and without the unemployment benefits the law requires of other employers.

The result is that both the employer and the parents ignore the child labor laws that were designed to protect children and to help ensure they have some kind of childhood in which to grow and mature. Boys like 17-year-old Fernando have no childhood, their chances of escaping the migrant poverty cycle are not good.

For many years Fernando's family has traveled north to Minnesota. They work eight weeks thinning and blocking sugar beets, chopping weeds, and thinning the unwanted plants with a hoe. When the beets are finished, the family moves into the cucumbers in Wisconsin. Fernando's father is sick with crippling arthritis and cannot work. The family is buying a small home in a colonia near Brownsville, Texas. Fernando is trying to finish high school and to help support the family.

In Texas, in the fall, he drives cotton-picking machines. "I have a lot of experience driving machines, I started driving tractor when I was 11.

"We were up in Minnesota and the farmer there, who knows the needs we have as a family, asked me if I wanted to drive a tractor. He told me if I worked a month and a half he would give me $250."

Young Fernando drove the tractor, discing and plowing, for only 30 days before the family had to leave for another area and another crop. Instead of $250 for 45 days, the farmer paid Fernando $150 for 30 days. That worked out to be 50 cents an hour.

Tractor work is dangerous. Had Fernando had any accidents?

"Once, but it wasn't a real accident. A disc on one side was kind of short [in close to the wheel]. I forgot about it. I turned and the disc went up over the wheel. I stopped the tractor and went over to the farmer. He was in the next field. He got real mad and he yelled, 'Goddamn, you know how much that's going to cost you? About $250. You don't make that kind of money!' Later he told me he was sorry, and didn't charge me for the tire. He let me keep driving. He told me he preferred tearing up the tire than to getting me killed."

The U.S. Department of Labor reports: "Though the figures on farm accidents are incomplete because most states do not cover farm employment accidents, and there is no national protection, the National Safety Council, newspaper stories, and some state reports verify that farm employment is the third most dangerous occupation, after mining and construction."

The National Safety Council statistics show 2,400 accidental deaths and 200,000 disabling injuries occurred on American farms in 1970. Tractors were a leading cause of death and injury. While there are no national statistics on injuries to children a 13-state study of 789 tractor fatalities found 12 percent of those killed were between 5 and 14 years old, too young to be legally driving or working around such machinery.

The Labor Department reported the gruesome details: "One Wisconsin boy, aged 10, was killed instantly and his 12- and 13-year-old brothers suffered arm and leg fractures and internal injuries when the 13-year-old lost control of the tractor while driving on loose gravel . . . .

"Other farm machinery also contributed to serious or fatal injuries. A 12-year-old boy had both arms ripped from his body when he was caught in a feed grinder. Another youth had his left hand so badly mangled when it caught in a corn picker, that amputation was required. And an 11-year-old boy was dead on arrival at the hospital two hours after falling into a bin of shelled corn while shoveling grain in the loft of the crib . . . ."[11]

The farm can be a very dangerous place for children.

2

Children work in the fresh and unpolluted open
air. They work in the early part of the day. They
work in the fresh fields, with flowers and birds
and wild life about them. What better environment
for children?

—An Oregon preacher

Jimmy's Dead

Jimmy Brooks died in the Philadelphia Chil-
dren's Hospital a week before his tenth birthday. Doctors there
diagnosed chemical pneumonitis, a lung disease thought to have
been caused by pesticides applied to a New Jersey tomato field.
For 48 days in the late summer of 1971, the doctors worked
hard to keep Jimmy alive. After his death the Philadelphia
Evening Bulletin reported: " . . . the child's lungs had been
destroyed by insecticide poisoning."

A week later New Jersey officials contradicted the attending
physicians; the official cause of death, following an autopsy,
was listed as a kidney disease. A state public health doctor
who had examined the medical records and the autopsy report
said: "The symptoms in this case in no way suggested pesticides."

New Jersey Secretary of Agriculture Philip Alampi wrote:
"Evidence which can be substantiated at this time gives no
indication that any laws of the state of New Jersey were violated

or that the death of [Jimmy Brooks] was directly caused by pesticides . . . ."

Both Alampi and Gabriel Coll, chief of the New Jersey Bureau of Migrant Labor, admitted their investigators failed to locate the Brooks family to talk to them, but Coll said interviews with other workers in the field revealed that "on no occasion was the field sprayed by the plane while the workers were thereon."

That is apparently as far as New Jersey officials must go. The state's pesticide application regulation protecting migrant farm workers reads: "Spraying or dusting with pesticides shall be prohibited at the time that the workers are harvesting crops on *that field*." I emphasize "that field" because Peter Brooks, Jimmy's father, told me the family was working in the cucumbers at the time and that the airplane was working an adjacent tomato field. He said the family was sprayed as the plane pulled up and turned at the end of each run.

The laws of New Jersey had not been violated and official state records listed death due to kidney disease. These reports troubled Dr. Leonard Bachman, the Children's Hospital physician who was in charge of Jimmy's case, and he continued the public argument: "It would be very risky and very radical to say that the death wasn't caused by spraying."

The doctor added his voice to the growing list of critics calling for stricter state control over the use of pesticides. And New Jersey officials angrily defended their position. When I questioned one state health doctor, he said: "I assume you suspect there might be a whitewash. I assure you there is no such intent. It was somewhat tragic-comic that a case that evokes such interest ended up nevertheless a spurious instance of poisoning . . . we have had other instances of pesticide poisoning among migrant workers that didn't receive the interest of this one . . . ."

The official reaction to the Brooks case made me want to learn more. I wanted to talk to the family to see how they lived, how they worked—and I wanted to learn more about how Jimmy died. It was only mid-September and Peter Brooks and his six surviving children should have been working somewhere in southern New Jersey. But heavy rains and poor growing conditions had wiped out the last few weeks of the season.

When I arrived in Bridgeton, many of the migrants were gone; the Brooks family was on its way back to Florida. So I followed the migrant stream south, into the Everglades country, into what was once a 15,000-square-mile swampland. It is now crisscrossed by great drainage canals, federally financed canals, that drain the swamps and allow the farmers to plow and plant the fertile black muck.

Farms in the 'Glades produce winter vegetables and the towns that lie south of Lake Okeechobee, towns like Pahokee, Belle Glade, Lake Harbor, and South Bay, are the winter home for thousands of Black migrant families.

The Brooks family lives in the crowded noisy heart of a Black ghetto. For $18 a week they rent a two-room apartment on the ground floor of a two-story building. From the outside it looks like a large, unpainted motel. Outside stairways and walkways lead to the rooms on the second floor. Inside, the apartments are small. The front room has a kitchen sink, a drainboard, and a two-burner stove along one wall; a small table, a double bed, and an army cot fill the rest of this room. The back room is even smaller.

Peter Brooks is sixty-one years old. He was born and raised in the then primitive swamp country around Lake Okeechobee. His father was a woodcutter who saw no need for his family to live in towns or for his children to go to school. They lived and worked a hard, primitive life, as remote from the white man as possible.

As "the 'Glades" were slowly converted from swamp to farmland—a conversion that has cost federal taxpayers $176 million to date—Peter Brooks drove tractors, planted crops, and harvested them. He moved with the shifting seasons. Florida farms supplied all the work he needed until he was thirty years old.

In 1941, after most of the work was finished in Florida's winter crops, Peter Brooks joined a crew that was going north "on the season," working East Coast croplands as far north as New York. They returned to Florida in the fall and Brooks was drafted into the Army, but was discharged four months later because he was illiterate.

We were sitting at the Brooks' kitchen table. The talk of his discharge brought conversation to an agonizing halt. His illiteracy embarrasses him. He fumbled out a pack of cigarettes, offered me one, lit his own, and coughed out the first deep drag, explaining, "I got the asthma real bad, so I smoke only the menthol kind."

Peter Brooks' face is aged and deeply wrinkled, like a prune withered too long in the hot sun. He is a slightly built, wiry man. There is little strength in his handshake, but the raspy feel of that calloused hand leaves no doubt he works for his living. His voice is soft and husky from too many cigarettes and sometimes his words are mumbled softly, self-consciously.

By the time Edward R. Murrow's CBS documentary film crews discovered and exposed the "Harvest of Shame" in 1962, Brooks was married and had seven children and had been "on the season" 20 years. In 1965 tragedy struck in Delaware. By then the Brooks family was traveling in their own car. One morning, as they pulled out of the labor camp on the way to work, another car struck theirs. Mrs. Brooks was killed.

At the time I talked to the family, only three of the children were back in school. John, 19, and Ann, 14, were at home. Al, who was just 16, had left home after a bitter argument with his father.

Peter Brooks started north for the summer of 1971 with six of his seven children. Jimmy was the youngest. In Virginia, their first stop, 9-year-olds can work legally. Brooks recalled, "We was in the beans and we could make $45, maybe $50 a day, but because there was too many people looking for work and because it was raining a lot, we was workin' maybe only two or three days a week.

"For two weeks there in Virginia we was in a camp only two nights. The rest of the time we was livin' out of the car. We'd eat by going to some lil' ol' store and buying cold cuts and soda pop, or we'd go to a cafe once in a while to get somethin' hot inside us."

They lived from hand to mouth, saving what they could. Brooks tries to find his own jobs, tries to avoid working for a crew leader. "Lots of 'em cheat ya, but even if they don't, the farmer may be payin' them 25 cents for tomatoes and you gettin' only 18, so you know the crew leader is gettin' rich, off of you."

In early July they moved on north, to New Jersey. "The year before we had been to one camp, but when we showed up this year, we found a bunch of Mexicans there, with their crew leader. So the farmer told us he don' have no place for us. We started off for Delaware. But we stopped by his brother's camp, to talk to some friends. They [someone from the other camp] called and asked if I thought I could get along with the Mexicans. I said I could. Them kind of people if you don't interfere with them, they ain't gonna bother you. So yeah, we got along fine. We moved in. It was on a Saturday or a Sunday."

The family was working picking beans and cucumbers. Sometimes they were offered a job clipping onions. "That's when we made our most money. Some weeks in the onions we [six workers] could get $180 or $200, but you always gotta work fast, because those onions don't last."

Was Jimmy working?

Brooks explained, "He wasn't old enough for the work law in New Jersey."

But Jimmy did "help out" when no one was watching, picking

first into one basket, then another. If he got tired he could rest or play, and then come back later to help.

Brooks said, ''I tell my children they are really blessed because in a lot of places they wouldn't even let them go out there in the field.

''One year in New York, if a child wasn't 15 or 16 they wouldn't even let him in the field. John there [he pointed to his 19-year-old son lounging on the army cot by the window], he remembers. That boy would lay down in the field so they couldn't see him. But if they [officials] did see him, he was most like a jack rabbit, the way he ran off and hid . . . .''

What happened July 14, 1971, the morning Jimmy was sprayed?

Brooks: ''We was working the cucumbers, me and the children, all except Jimmy. This morning he wanted to pick some, and he did work a while, but then he went to the car 'cause he said he was sleepy.

''The airplane come over about the time Jimmy got to sleep. It come over six times—four times from north to south. He [the pilot] was spraying a block of tomatoes, the wind was blowin' our way. He'd start on the back side and work to us. Every time he'd make a flight, he'd come close to the car . . . the wind was blowing and the wind from the plane shoved that stuff a long ways. He made about four [passes] round down on the tomato field—there must of been 45 or 50 rows of 'matoes on this side of the [farm] house and there was some trees.

''He went down and around and come over the end of the cucumber field to finish gettin' that by where the trees and the house was. By the time he got through sprayin' that way the boy woke up and he got out of the car and come over to us.

''By the time Jimmy got over to us, the pilot made two

more passes right across the north end of the cucumber field and we all had to duck down, you know?''

Could you feel the spray? See it?

"Yeah, you could sure feel it, and see it. Just like somebody throw up a bucket of water and it come down on you . . . ."

Ann, the 14-year-old daughter, had joined us at the table and had been listening. She is a quiet, shy girl. I asked her the same question. "Yes sir, I did. We could see it, too. It was the color of the milk there, but a bit more yellow. I'll show you what was in it."

She got up from the table and went out the front door. Since her mother's death, Ann had taken over her duties, she kept track of the bills, did the family shopping. Her own life was getting more complicated, she had a boyfriend and she was pregnant. She wanted to finish school, but the future didn't look too promising.

Ann came back in and handed me a piece of paper on which the Philadelphia doctor had written three words: "Malthion," "Sevin," and "Maneb."

These are common farm chemicals—two are pesticides that attack the nervous sytem and one is a fungicide.

Both Ann and her father said the residues of the spray could be seen on the car and they knew some of the material remained on them.

But Brooks explained, "We didn't figure the pilot would be puttin' out anything that would hurt us. He could see we was workin' this end of the field and the Mexicans was workin' on the other end. I don't know if he got down that way to them or not."

The family finished its work in the cucumber field about midmorning and moved to another field to clip onions. The father explained, "After awhile I see Jimmy was goin' out to the bushes to hisself, and I asked one of the children—I think it was Charles Lee or maybe Willie—anyway

I asked one of them why Jimmy was runnin' out there so much and they say he was heavin'—you know, throwin' up.

"I thought he had been eatin' something so I went an' asked him if he felt bad. He said, 'no,' but about 1 o'clock I looked at him and his face is swelled up. I wasn't feelin' too good myself, so about 3 p.m. I figured maybe I ought to take Jimmy to the doctor."

According to Brooks, a Bridgeton doctor diagnosed either an allergy or asthma, gave them "some pink pills," and told them to bring Jimmy back the next day.

That was Wednesday, July 14. Jimmy saw the doctor the next day and seemed to be improving Friday and Saturday. "Sunday morning we had some beans to pick. I called Jimmy and he got up. He started vomiting. He said his head was hurting and said something about he had the asthma. We went out to the field, but we left Jimmy in the car 'cause he wasn't feelin' well.

"We picked until about 8:30 or 9 o'clock and then went back to the car. The kids tried to get Jimmy up, but they couldn't so they just pushed him over so they could climb in. When we got to the camp, I told Jimmy to get out, but he was sluggish, like he couldn't, so I helped him . . . ." Brooks dressed Jimmy in clean clothes and they drove to the hospital in Bridgeton, arriving at 11 a.m.

Telling about trying to get Jimmy admitted to the hospital made Brooks angry. "It took them from 11 a.m. to 1 o'clock to make up their minds what they were going to do. They look at Jimmy, they feel him, they ax me a thousand questions, then go right back over those questions again.

"Had I ever brought him to the hospital before, ever been real sick before . . . I was about wore out with those people.

"If I had known anywhere else to carry Jimmy, I'd have moved him, but I didn't know nowheres else. I didn't know how bad off he was; ever once in a while he would raise up his head . . . ."

Tears came to Brooks' eyes. He stopped, lit another menthol cigarette, and started coughing.

In moments like this I saw a very lonely man trapped in a senseless, cruel maze of circumstance. How does anyone learn to cope with a series of events like those that led up to Jimmy's death?

Peter Brooks dislikes migrant life, he feels it harms his children. But he can see no way out. "The kids is out of school, they is around the camps, they see a lot of sex an' gamblin' and fightin' and they don' know if it is wrong or not, so a boy he just gonna do what he sees everybody else doin'. So you see kids 8 and 9 gamblin' . . . ."

John agreed: "Yeah, well really. Yeah, that's what happens . . . ."

Peter: "They go out there in the woods [outside camp] and get to messin' round, be a game [of cards or craps] or somethin' else [whore]. Some of them [youngsters] pick only three or four hours then they scoot off out there in the woods . . . ."

John is a dark-chocolate-colored, muscular youth with a fine mustache. He split off from the family during the summer months to work and travel on his own with another crew. He worked up into Pennsylvania with a crew leader who was "a pretty nice guy," but found "there wasn't no money to be made. We was just beginning to make some money in the tomatoes, you know, when it came a late rain. The rains wiped out the best pickin's."

How much money did he come home with?

Peter Brooks laughed, cutting his son off. "He didn't save nothing. If I hadn't been up there you wouldn't a got back at all."

John: "He's right. Seems like the whole season there hasn't been nothin'. It was bad here last winter before we took off, so bad they give us [the family] disaster checks. Then this summer wasn't nothin' at all.''

I asked Ann if she would work in the fields this winter with John and her father.

"No, I want to go back to school.''

But because of her pregnancy she had already delayed going back to enroll, busying herself instead with the household chores.

How long had Ann been going north?

"As long as I can remember.'' She seldom volunteered any information, but would quietly, seriously respond to all my questions.

Her favorite state?

"Delaware.''

Why?

"I like the school, I like math and to create things. I liked Delaware because I went to summer school there. It was a real big school . . . .''

Ann misses her mother. As she works about the sink or stove or looks up a telephone number or address for her father, she is moving in her mother's footsteps. Because she had to begin assuming this role when Jimmy was only three, she became as much mother as sister to the boy.

She recalls, ''Jimmy was full of it, always gettin' into things, always a goin'. Whenever he'd get home from school first place he'd head would be to watch 'em [Little Leaguers] play baseball. He wanted to play so bad. Baseball was his favorite.''

It was difficult for Brooks to talk about Jimmy's final weeks. Jimmy was transferred almost immediately from the Bridgeton, New Jersey, hospital to Philadelphia Children's Hospital. The family continued to work in the fields, making the two or three hour drive into the city to visit Jimmy when they could. But the boy was never fully conscious. He was in a respirator and extremely weak.

Brooks said, ''They [the doctors] warned me that he did

not have much of a chance to recover. He was in a lot of pain. You could call and he wouldn't talk, but we'd ask if he knew who was talking and he'd nod his head.''

On the father's last visit to the hospital before returning the other children to school in Florida, Jimmy was unconscious. Brooks said, ''His pulse was weak, and I give him up then.''

Jimmy Brooks died before his father could return from Florida.

The attending physician, Dr. Leonard Bachman, said the boy had been admitted to the Children's Hospital with both a severe lung condition and a secondary kidney involvement. At the time of admission the doctors learned from the father that Jimmy had been sprayed by an airplane.

Curiously, this is the first mention of pesticide exposure in the boy's medical records. I asked Dr. Bachman if the father had volunteered the information.

He said, ''I don't know if the intake workers asked about spray or pesticides or poisoning, but they could have. We probably are a little more thorough about trying to dig out the history here.''

It is hard for a city dweller to understand how the father could fail to mention something as dramatic as a low-flying airplane spraying poisons. But to farm workers a low-flying crop duster is a routine sight. Sometimes the planes fly directly over the workers and the spray falls on them. They have no way of knowing what the chemicals are. They may get a bit of a rash, a headache. Once in a while some of them get sick and vomit, but the sickness goes away.

Most farm workers across the nation have very little idea of what pesticide dangers they face. There is little connection in their minds between the illnesses they suffer and the airplanes or ground-spray rigs. So when Peter Brooks took his sick son to the doctor nothing very dramatic had occurred. Also, Brooks is a Black man, an illiterate migrant seeking the help of the white man.

Dr. Bachman explained the diagnosis: "The kind of lung disease he had can be caused by what we call chemical irritants, say smoke inhalation. We have seen this kind of condition with kerosene poisoning. This kind of condition that [Jimmy] had in those first days, what seemed to kill him, was very typical of that kind of thing and we call it chemical pneumonitis.

"In investigating the sprays, we found none of the constituents of the sprays had been known to cause their toxic effect in that manner. Although chemicals close to their kind of chemicals do it.

"So we worked on the idea that, hell, we don't know what was in that spray. We don't know that even the research work is that good on that kind of constituents and we don't know if an overwhelming dose might have caused that, and we went on to think that was what had caused the thing . . . ."

The first news accounts came after Jimmy's death; and, because pesticides are a controversial subject within the environmental-ecology arguments, the stories were picked up by the wires.

When Dr. Robert Segul, Philadelphia's assistant medical examiner, did the autopsy and reported that kidney disease was the probable cause of death, New Jersey officials used the report to beat back critics of their pesticide policies.

The two doctors, Segul and Bachman, were not antagonistic toward each other. They were like men working on the same large puzzle; each had been given a handful of pieces to fit in place, but nothing fit snugly and, in the end, when each man had contributed his share, they found so many pieces still missing no picture emerged clearly.

Dr. Bachman concluded, "If, indeed, the boy was sprayed, I would say you would have to bet on it being some irritant in the spray that caused the lung trouble . . . ."

The New Jersey state public health doctor who saw the "tragic-comic" effects in the case insisted pesticides had nothing to do with the case. He said, "The insecticides allegedly used, we don't have known toxicity, we don't know how much is enough to kill somebody. But that isn't the point. The point is someone could have been lying; in the more toxic pesticides the symptoms come on within hours, often within two hours. The symptoms in this case in no way suggested pesticides . . . ."

It is easy to get sidetracked in such a controversy because so little is known about the effects of pesticides on farm workers. Throughout the nation there is an amazing lack of regulation over the sale, storage, and use of these chemicals on the farm. Congress gives the U.S. Department of Agriculture $180 million a year in research funds to help farmers fight their war against bugs; only $160,000 of this is spent developing safer ways to handle these deadly poisons.[1]

It is presumed the growers and the appliers they hire have the knowledge and the skill to use these chemicals safely. Yearly this presumption has been fatal to hundreds and injurious to thousands. Farm workers have little protection against the effects of pesticides. They may be sprayed accidentally from the air or the ground, they may brush through poisonous residues on the plant foliage as they work, they may inhale the residues that collect in the dust.

The workers' most immediate threat comes from the phosphate and carbamate pesticides that closely resemble the World-War-II nerve gasses. These fast-acting chemicals attack the nervous system by destroying a body enzyme called cholinesterase. Cholinesterase is a catalyst essential to the electrochemical transmission of nerve impulses that regulate the functions of vital body organs.

A single drop of any of the most toxic phosphate pesticides kills within minutes or hours. The mildest of these poisons, absorbed as the worker passes through the field, may never be noticed.

But as a worker's body absorbs even mild quantities of the poison the supply of cholinesterase is depleted. With each exposure a small amount of the enzyme is destroyed. The effect is cumulative as long as exposure continues. As the cholinesterase supply is depressed an insidious set of symptoms begins to appear. The worker feels as if he is getting the flu or a cold; he may have a headache, be dizzy and sick to his stomach. He may develop a rash or have double vision.

If the exposure is eliminated, the body rebuilds the cholinesterase supply and the symptoms disappear. If exposure continues, the supplies of cholinesterase continue to fall until a crisis is reached: The body's vital organs receive chaotic, garbled orders; malfunctions appear in the form of critical illness or death.

Malathion and Sevin, the pesticides used in the tomato field next to where the Brooks family worked, are cholinesterase-depressing chemicals. They have known toxic properties. In California, fields sprayed by a Malathion-Sevin combination are considered too dangerous for workers to reenter for three days. After that the chemicals have broken down into harmless residues.

California is one of the few states to have worker-protection regulations for all agriculture chemicals. These regulations establish "safe reentry times" for all pesticides applied individually or in combination; the limits range from one day for the mildest of these economic poisons to up to 45 days for some applications of the highly toxic and unpredictable pesticides like Parathion.

The phosphates and carbamates are now widely used because in addition to their quick deadliness, they go through rapid chemical decomposition. The DDT family of chlorinated hydrocarbons were excellent bug killers, and once applied, they continued to work for long periods of time. At first, this residual effect—and their apparent nontoxic effect on workers—made the DDT-type pesticides the safest and most desirable of the pesticides.

But DDT's long life, its ability to pass upward through the food chain from plant to animal in increasingly concentrated forms, has made it environmentally unacceptable.

As the state and federal governments began to restrict the use of the chlorinated hydrocarbons, the farmers were forced to use the shorter-lived, more deadly phosphates and carbamates.

This switch was like stepping onto a chemical treadmill. Because these pesticides had such a short life, they had to be applied more often and the more often they were applied, the faster bugs developed immunities. This called for more deadly chemicals and the environment for workers became increasingly more dangerous. But the emphasis has remained on developing more deadly bug killers, not protecting workers.

How many men, women, and children are killed or injured by pesticides yearly? The U.S. Senate Migratory Labor Subcommittee tried to find out in 1969. At the time the Food and Drug Administration was spending $14 million on a pesticide research program that it had started in 1965. After four years of work the FDA investigators could establish proof of only 150 to 200 pesticide deaths in the nation each year. They estimated there were at least four times that many, but because so few states kept any kind of farm labor occupational health reports, there were no accurate figures.

An FDA official told the senators that for every death, they estimated 100 accidental poisonings that resulted in loss of time from work. Under questioning by Senator Walter Mondale the witness agreed that it was possible that up to 800 workers died a year and that 80,000 more were injured by pesticides. Such estimates and reluctant admissions of "possibilities" are so vague and so susceptible to argument they are meaningless as specific information.

However, the figures and the circumstance in which they were projected do indicate a serious problem exists. There are other indicators that are less vague, but almost as inconclusive. In California, Dr. Thomas Milby, chief of the Occupational Health Division, California Department of Public Health, directed a study of 774 farm workers of all ages to find how many might have a history of phosphate pesticide exposure. Twenty percent of the sample had five or more of the flu-like symptoms characteristic of cholinesterase depression.

There are 1,400 farm worker pesticide poisoning cases a year confirmed in California; most of these workers recover, but 9 or 10 die. Over a 16-year period there have been 151 pesticide deaths; 85 percent of these were children under 16 years old. These statistics, plus the state's investigation of pesticide problems, caused Dr. Milby to comment, "It is our belief that a major, yet unsolved problem in occupational disease has to do with pesticides. We have to find the extent of the problem, identify the chemicals involved, and design preventative protections."

The job is awesome. There are an estimated 800 pesticide compounds and they are formulated into 60,000 brand name products. Each chemical company dispatches large sales forces into the farmers' fields, each company spends large sums on radio, television, and newspaper advertising. The message: "Bugs chew up profits, so kill the bugs—before they eat up the farm." The result is overkill.

As early as 1951 farm workers were reported poisoned by the highly toxic Parathion. This is a broad-spectrum phosphate pesticide that will kill almost anything. In Delano, California, a vineyardist applied Parathion 33 days before the workers were to start thinning. At the time, the grower followed all the rules and regulations, yet 16 of the 25 workers became ill. They were sent to the hospital where it was discovered they suffered from cholinesterase depression. All survived.

In 1958 the Journal of the American Medical Association reported 11 cases of Parathion poisoning involving 70 people working in pears, apples, grapes, citrus, and hops. The workers picked up the poison as they brushed through the foliage. Throughout the 1950's and 1960's other reports filtered in through medical journals and county health department records.

A Mississippi 16-year-old was handling a Parathion spray boom as someone else drove the tractor. The boy was furnished no protective clothing or respirator. A report reads: "The boy was rushed to the hospital, but was not admitted, due to alleged administrative delay. He was later taken to another hospital where he was DOA [dead on arrival]."

In South Carolina a 15-year-old boy was mixing Parathion solution for a spray plane when he splashed some on his clothes. He took off his shirt, but didn't wash thoroughly. Doctors at a nearby hospital managed to save his life. But a 14-year-old boy working in Ohio was not so fortunate; he died after accidentally inhaling Parathion dust. He had no protective gear and was illegally employed. (The Fair Labor Standards Act identifies handling of pesticides as a hazardous job and workers must be 16 years old to work around these chemicals.)

A Rio Grande Valley newspaper reported that fourteen Mexican-American farmhands were felled by Parathion sprayed on a cotton field where they worked. Three nearly died before responding to treatment. In 1963 a California farm worker died and 94 others were seriously poisoned as they picked peaches in Stanislaus County. The weather had been unusually hot, the workers were sweating freely, and many of the men had taken off their shirts.

There should have been no danger. The grower had applied Parathion several weeks before, and he had followed the directions and taken the safety precautions required.

Dr. Milby sent a team of investigators into the area. In addition to checking those who were originally reported, Dr. Milby's staff went into nearby orchards, testing other workers. There were widespread signs of cholinesterase depression. Workers were complaining of headaches, dizziness, double vision, nausea, and vomiting.

No one could explain what happened. Chemical analysis of the residues found on the peach tree leaves showed the Parathion had gone through the first stages of degradation, turning into the more deadly concentrate called paroxon. But there the degradation inexplicably stopped.

Several times in the ensuing years similar incidents have happened in California fruit orchards. Each time the cases are studied, men are puzzled, and the state agriculture department revises its "safe reentry time," making the workers stay out of the fields for longer periods.

Despite such dramatic evidence of toxicity, there is a strange, rather cavalier attitude expressed by some public officials toward pesticides. In Florida two state legislators were arguing against proposed pesticide regulations.

One said, "I don't know that anybody's been killed by touching them."

The other legislator agreed. "I haven't heard much about why we need to control pesticides."

Their conversation was printed in the Miami *Herald*. Further on in the same story it was reported Florida has had 428 pesticide poisonings and 7 deaths reported annually "and health officials admit their records don't reflect all the poisonings." Most of the victims are children below the age of 10.

Newspaper accounts of poisonings are not popular in rural areas; if an argument is made against the use of pesticides, the agri-business community responds with a counterattack. One major chemical company withdrew advertising from a newspaper that ran stories explaining the dangers of pesticides. County farm advisors and pesticide regulation officials labeled the articles false and emotionally misleading and went right on with the system that puts all of the control in the hands of appliers and growers.

Field workers like Peter Brooks believe the farmers would not apply anything that would harm the workers. They do not equate the skin rashes, the eye irritations, the sniffles and flu-like feelings directly with the airplane in a nearby field. Farm workers bring "the stuff" home to use on roaches and rats.

One mother told me how her husband brought home an empty can, rinsed it out well, and set it out on the porch to dry. Their 18-month-old baby "got to playin' with the can, maybe licked a drop out of it, or something. In less than two hours she was dead."

A field worker told this horror story: "The bugs were eating up the greens that I was growing in my yard. I told my neighbor this and he gave me some of the powdered stuff and told me to throw it on the ground around my plants . . . the powdered stuff smelled like the stuff they use in the fields to spray the plants [where he worked]."

This man was lucky. Two weeks later, when the family ate the greens, no one got sick, the residues were harmless by this time. Sometime later he heard about seven children dying of Parathion poison and told a friend he had never seen Parathion.

The friend couldn't believe his ears. "Man, that stuff you been putting out was Parathion."[2]

An 18-year-old working with his family reported: "A plane flew over the field we were working in and sprayed us with some chemical made of little pellets that were white. The plane sprayed us with stuff in the field from one o'clock to about four thirty, when it quit for the day.

"Most of the people complained of headaches that day and about the fumes from the stuff. I was dizzy. I wanted to quit, but I was afraid to because they get mad if you quit. When we got home that night, my father's back was all broken out and the next day it was covered with bleeding sores. He lost several days of work . . . ."[3]

Work is what farm workers can least afford to lose, so they seldom complain, seldom make trouble. Most expect to be sick, at least part of the time. Few understand the insidious nature of the cholinesterase-depression symptoms.

The flu, the colds, the dizziness are just illnesses you live with. Sometimes, when they are in fields without pesticide residues, their health is good, the work is enjoyable, maybe it's spring and it feels good to be alive.

But when they go into a nearby field that has been sprayed—or an airplane sprays a field off a ways and the wind carries the pesticides over to them—the good feelings begin to disappear. The conditions affect the children, too, but no one knows quite how.

Dr. Lee Mizrahi, a pediatrician who has established a farm worker medical clinic in the San Joaquin Valley, ran some cholinesterase blood tests, as part of a larger study of farm worker children.

"Of the 58 children studied, we found 27 had abnormally low cholinesterase levels when compared to normal values which are established for adults," the doctor said, adding, "When I began to ask scientists what these low levels meant, I was told that our clinic was the first in the United States to analyze rural children's blood in this manner. To me it is tragically absurd that in 1969 such a study by an obscure rural doctor should be the first ever done on children . . . ."

3

Farm laborers can earn $40 to $50 a day [but] many migrant workers, once being paid off at this high rate, will not work again until their money runs out . . . [too many] prefer to sit back and accept the dole . . . [taxpayers'] dollars are being used to support those who can help themselves but are not willing to do so.

—*Senator Spessard Holland*

On the Season

Torrential rains fell across south Florida. The downpour returned the black earth to swampland, crops were beaten into the muck, then flooded. Water stood everywhere.

Newspapers reported: "Farmers watched their vegetable crops drown, cattle waded through water in search of food and canals gushed the runoff into the sea . . . .

"Rainfall that is 20 times normal for March left the Collier county truck farmers with less than a 30 percent crop prospect for the third crop of the 1969–70 season . . . ."

It had been a disastrous winter for the farmers. The first two crops were damaged by unseasonal freezing and by rains. Then in early March the rain started again. It slowed the celery harvest because the cutters had to watch for mold and blight. The rains continued and all work had to be stopped.

During the last week of March and the first week of April the damage was assessed and reported in the local press.

Florida's governor asked the federal government to declare a disaster in the area so farmers could qualify for federal assistance. This was high drama, man against the elements with millions of dollars riding in the balance. The farmers had dared to make the gamble and now they were losing.

Such tableaux are a part of the nation's heritage, a part of the myths grown up around the family farm. But behind this public drama of the rugged farmer standing alone there is always another less popular story of disaster. Floods put farm workers out of work, but they have not risked great sums of money, their only losses are food and shelter for themselves and their families. When the story of their privation and suffering is belatedly brought into public view it is almost never popular; such exposures generate more passionate argument than action.

In the spring of 1970, as official disaster status was being requested for farmers, the Florida Rural Manpower Service was reporting a "lull in the citrus harvest," "underemployment in the vegetables," and that "heavy rains over the weekend interfered with the use of workers."

The phraseology of the last sentence suggests the agri-business attitude. Workers are used and then put aside until needed again and they are expected to remain silent while not in use. There are about 110,000 migrant workers in Florida for the winter harvests, 40,000 of them are school-age children who must work 15 to 18 hours a week if their families are to survive during normal times.

On April 3, 1970, the Palm Beach *Post* reported: "State agencies are not aiding agricultural workers out of work as a result of heavy rainfall and crop failure, migrant legal service personnel in south Florida claimed yesterday."

Elijah Boone, a Florida Rural Legal Service investigator and former migrant worker told the *Post* that only 4 or 5 bus loads of workers were going to the fields daily from Belle Glade's Loading Ramp. Normally 30 to 40 buses carry workers out from this predawn shapeup in the heart of Belle Glade's ghetto.

By the second week in April newspapers were carrying stories about legal service attorneys and young Black and Chicano militants protesting the government inaction. The Florida Council of Churches estimated 70,000 people were out of work. The protestors claimed the local, state, and federal bureaucrats were more concerned about flooded farms, cattle, and wild deer herds than about hungry people. Hungry farm worker families marched on the Collier County courthouse to demonstrate their plight.

Across the state the mayor of Belle Glade accused the Florida Rural Legal Services of bringing in outside agitators to stir up trouble: "Some instances of poverty and unemployment do exist here, but there has not been a great increase. And until the day of the demonstration the welfare office reported no great increase in people applying for help there."

Such controversy is not new, nor is it unique to Florida. Throughout the farm states there is a continuing conflict of interests. The farmer, with thousands of dollars in debts hanging over his maturing crop, wants to be assured of an adequate labor supply, and he wants the workers to be in his area ahead of time so they will be available if a sudden hot spell brings the crop on earlier than expected. Over-recruitment results and the work force arrives a week or more before the crop is ready. If the crop is late in maturing the workers wait, without pay.

These workers must have jobs to survive. When they are out of work their meager reserves shrink rapidly and they must seek assistance. Here the farm community reacts in puzzling ways. An Ohio farmer, asked a general question about the quality of migrant work, replied: "They worked hard until we got the food stamp program up here and this has been a bad hurt . . . lot of 'em work no more than they have to to get food stamps, then they say 'to hell with you' and they slow down . . . ."

Collier County, Florida, uses 18,000 to 22,000 migrants a year. Reports of hunger and malnutrition in the county prompted the U.S. Senate Select Committee on Nutrition and Human Needs to hold hearings there in 1969. Senator George McGovern, the committee chairman, asked Collier County Commissioner Ewell Moore if the commissioner had been quoted accurately in a newspaper.

The quote reads: "If the federal people are going to do it [feed the hungry] O.K. The migrants themselves are federal people. They are not Immokalee people. They are not Collier County people. They are not Florida people. If there is free food these people'll come early and stay late. We'll have them in town all year long."

Moore answered McGovern: "No sir, I didn't say that exactly, but I almost concur with every word of it."

Immokalee newspaper editor Stan Wrisley testified that farmers in the area could not get enough workers to go into the fields. "It is not because people are not here, not because people are too hungry to work, but because they don't want to work for $10 or $15 a day, because they can get welfare without work."

Such attitudes are common in rural America. Coolies, peons, boys, Okies, and harvest hands are generally believed incapable of living in a decent house without tearing it up, so decent housing is not justified; it is said these people do not know how to spend their money wisely, that they drink and fight and have illegitimate babies to cheat the welfare system out of tax dollars.

The prejudices and stereotypes are so heavy and so pervasive the words "Negro" and "Mexican" have taken on pejorative meanings. Children begin to believe they are dumb niggers and dirty Mexicans and poor white trash. In the words of one county politician, "They are just farm workers, that's all they are and that's all they ever will be."

It isn't difficult to trace the origins of such stereotypes. In Florida they obviously are rooted in slavery. When the slaves were freed, the sharecrop and the tenant-farm systems were devised to work the land and earn a profit for the plantation owner. Farm work was hand and mule labor and the rights of ownership prevailed.

The benevolent owner always cared for his mules and his workers—as long as they remained in quiet servitude. But the increased cost of production required more efficient forms of power to sustain profit margins. The mule and the tenant farmer were no longer profitable.

From Alabama and Mississippi and Georgia, the sharecroppers and tenant farmers and their families were forced off the land. They sought work where they could find it, they became migrants. Many ''went North'' into New York and New Jersey seasonally and returned home to the South to live on what they had earned. But it was never enough. In the 1930's and '40's, as the federal government aided the farmers in draining the Florida Everglades, work in the winter vegetable crops and citrus groves became available. Florida became the East Coast migrants' winter home. Florida farmers needed these workers. They recruited throughout the South, trying to attract the landless Black families.

For Mrs. Laurine Pickett the shift from poverty on a tenant farm to the rootless, hungry life of a migrant child occurred in the 1950's when she was 7. Mrs. Pickett recalled: ''My father had a pretty good farm in Georgia. We were runnin' it on shares and we were the only family living on The Man's place. Once a year, at Christmas time, my father used to go up to the big house to settle up, to collect what profits there were after The Man deducted the farming costs and what he had advanced us to live on.

''I can remember the last two or three years before we left, my father would come walkin' back, his head down.

''He'd be kicking at the dust, or an old can. Sometimes he'd pick up a rock an' throw it and his face—you could see the hurt and anger. My mother would ask what had happened and he would shrug and say, 'We ended up in the hole again this year.'

"I was just small then, but I remember trying to help mother chop cotton. We [four children] all tried to help. We would go to school a couple of days and we would stay home a couple of days.

"My father was always trying to find an outside job to help us get along. Sometimes he'd get a day or two of work, but there wasn't much to do in those parts. The farmer, he would advance us $15 every two weeks to live on. My father would hunt squirrels and rabbits. Oh, he'd scuffle real hard to keep us eating.

"The Man could see how hard up we was, so he let us have a patch to grow vegetables. We'd all of us work the garden, and if we see any bottles or scrap along the road, we'd save it. We'd do all we could to keep from using The Man's money. We all worked so hard at it we kind of got silly about savin' and scrimpin'. Then come the last of November and Father went up to settle up, we all just knowin' he had something coming. But he came back, his head hanging. A whole year, and we hadn't made nothin'. I can remember bein' so mad and hurt, because we were a part of it, too, you know.

"We had an aunt, living in Belle Glade, in a camp, and my father wanted to take us to her. But we had no way, the ol' truck he had wouldn't hold together that far, an' there was no money for gas or food.

"But my father made a plan. We planted that whole vegetable patch to cucumbers and when they was ready, he got us all up, really early, and we'd pick cucumbers and load them on that ol' truck. He'd take them to town, before the farmer was up and about, so he wouldn't know we was trying to save some cash money.

"My father saved every penny of that, but when he saw it wasn't going to be enough, he got up at 3 a.m., loaded the truck with all the corn he could get into it, and he drove off to Alabama. Four mornings he stole all the corn he could stuff into that truck. He told us not to say anything, he said The Man really owed us something, and we was just taking what was ours.

"He used the money for bus tickets to get us all out. My mother was scared, because there were a lot of stories about what a farmer would do if he caught you stealing and running.

"My mother was real sad the morning we left. She had to choose what she could take. Father would only let us carry a single suitcase. When we were all packed, my father loaded us into the truck and, before dawn, drove us out to the highway where the bus stopped. We all hid down there in the bushes, while Father drove the truck back to the farm, and came out to us. He gave a whistle when he saw the bus and we all come out."

They escaped to Belle Glade. They were migrant workers now. Each spring they traveled north, with a labor contractor, riding the shoddy buses. Each winter they were back in Belle Glade.

Mrs. Pickett recalls: "In the winter, in Florida, we would try to go to school, but Father would pull us out sometimes to help him make it. We would try to explain that we couldn't miss school because there was a test, or something, and he would just tell us we had to pay the rent. We would all go pick beans, and if we made enough one day, we could go back to school the next."

As Mrs. Pickett talked, she drove me through the Black sections of Belle Glade, South Bay, and Pahokee, showing me where the farm workers lived, introducing me to some of the families.

Belle Glade is the unofficial winter capital of the Black migrant farm workers. In the summer the city's population is 17,000, but in the winter, after all the migrants have returned from their northern trek, there are 30,000 people living in the city. The new arrivals crowd into the Black ghetto.

In Florida they call it the "agri-ghetto." It is an old, decaying part of town. The balconies on the two-story buildings hang out over the sidewalk, crowding the streets. In the unbearable hot, humid fall, few people stay indoors. Out along the balconies and walkways, Black mothers hang out their wash or sit, spraddle-legged, on old kitchen chairs, fanning themselves and sipping soda.

Infants, their white diapers contrasting with their dark skin, toddle along; older children scramble up and down the stairways, yelling, throwing things, crying. Down on the streets cars choke the narrow traffic lanes; here and there a big delivery truck double parks, blocking the traffic. Horns honk, people shout, music from the tavern juke boxes fills the air. Men lounge in doorways, shopkeepers stand outside, talking, smoking, spitting in the gutters. Young dudes in Afro hair styles strut the streets, eyeing the sexy girls in their tight pants and braless blouses.

In this overcrowded ghetto a family of five pays $50 to $60 a month for a two- or three-room "apartment." Half the available rentals have no toilet or bath and a third have no indoor plumbing or water supply at all. These apartments are little more than wooden or concrete block cells. In those that do have indoor plumbing, the toilets are broken, the faucets and sinks leak. Rats and roaches are a constant irritant.

Just outside the central ghetto, out in the back lots, alleys, and sidestreets there is an incredible array of decaying shanties, wooden hovels that rent as single-family dwellings. They sag. They lean. They tilt. Some have pit privies, others have no toilet facility at all. The tenants of such places must use slop jars and a shovel.

When work starts in the fall, the streets of Belle Glade are less crowded. Each morning, before dawn, thousands of men, women, and children gather at the Loading Ramp, a large square between Fifth and Sixth Streets near the heart of the ghetto. There, 30 or 40 buses are parked and crew leaders stand beside them, calling off the work that is available. Each crew leader has contracted to plant, or cultivate, or harvest a farmer's crops, and to accomplish the promised work he recruits daily at places like the Loading Ramp.

The only protection the worker has is the word-of-mouth reputation each crew leader has earned. Only about half of these labor contractors are registered, as required by the federal crew leader act. However, there is little time spent worrying about this Congressional attempt to regulate crew leaders. Enforcement of the law has been practically nonexistent.

The scene at the Loading Ramp is like the dock workers shape-up. The crew leader's selection processes are his own, however; there are no unions to regulate the procedure. The crew leader's choices may be directed by caprice, by spite, by avarice, or simply by the need to find workers willing to labor for the wage he is offering.

There are school-age children among the daily shapeup. By the time the cool is off the morning, these youngsters are 20 to 30 miles away from classrooms, teachers, and truant officers. Once they are in the field they are committed to the long, hard day of work. There is no way back to town except by the crew leader's bus; wages and working conditions in the field are not necessarily those promised back there in the haste of Loading Ramp recruitment.

About one-third of the parents take their school-age children to the field with them, sometimes. Their school attendance is dictated by the family's need and that need shifts from day to day as the rent comes due or as the supplies of food dwindle. Work is never steady, so the children learn early to help their parents. By the time the migrant child is 12, he or she is working from 16 to 18 hours a week. Not long afterward most drop out of school altogether.

These facts were revealed in the Florida Migrant Child Survey conducted by Professor John Kleinert of the University of Miami. Kleinert said: "Quite frequently the children go into the fields with their parents to assist them so as to increase [family] productivity. [By] keeping parents supplied with picking sacks and baskets [children] give the parents more time to pick . . . as the children become older, they assume the role of the full-fledged worker."

Kleinert's statewide study, funded by the Florida State Department of Education in an effort to learn more about migrant children, revealed statistically that 56 percent of the migrant families were Black. The rest were Spanish-speaking—from Mexico, Texas, Puerto Rico, and Cuba. Only a few were Anglo.

Most of Florida's migrants live within the agri-ghettos of towns like Belle Glade that ring the south end of Lake Okeechobee and the east coast towns that extend from West Palm Beach south to Miami. Most (62 percent) have both the mother and father living and working within the family unit. The great majority of the families want to stop migrating and to settle down.

But settling down is out of the question. Miami *Herald* staff writer John K. deGroot wrote: "For 53,539 men and women of the fields it is impossible to find year-round employment in the sunshine state."

This was the lead paragraph on one of six stories deGroot wrote on migrants. The Florida Fruit and Vegetable Association singled the series out, labeling it "extremely objective reporting." The series then should be a fair representation of the agri-business community's views. DeGroot labeled the farm worker housing within the cities "agri-ghettos" and pointed out the plumbing and sanitation shortcomings. He exposed the acute housing shortage throughout south central Florida that had forced rent higher as living conditions went from bad to worse.

According to deGroot there are 400 private labor camps in Florida and 40 percent of these camps fail to meet even the minimal public health and safety standards. While such statistics convey objective facts, they tend to understate the horror of some 12,000 people living in 160 substandard labor camps.

I inspected several of these private camps. In one large camp there were row upon row of 15-foot square wooden boxes. The cabins were old, the wood was decaying. They were of single-wall construction, sheeted over with tarpaper and set up off the muck on cement or wooden blocks. Besides having two windows and one door the only "amenity" within these boxes was a single electric light socket hung from the roof ridge pole.

Each interior was divided in half by a wall that extended from the back almost to the front door. The wall was only six feet high. A narrow shelf was installed on the wall, directly below the light socket, and the shelf was sheathed in tin to allow for use of a hot plate or kerosene stove. In one of the cabins charred wood showed where a fire had broken out above the stove but had been quickly extinguished.

Fires are a constant danger in such camps. In February of 1969 three infants burned to death in a fire that destroyed the 15-by-20-foot cabin they were staying in. The fire was started by a kerosene cook stove being used by a 10-year-old who was caring for six children. The parents were at work in the fields.

Fire isn't the only health hazard. Pit privies contaminate nearby shallow wells; ancient, leaking plumbing fouls the areas around the central washhouses and shower rooms. Garbage disposal is a serious problem in remote areas; rats and cockroaches thrive in many of these camps.

There are some modern, clean-looking, private farm labor housing developments. Some of the large two-story barracks built by the big sugar cane growers to house imported "offshore" cane cutters are impressive. Each year these companies import several thousand male Jamaican and Puerto Rican cane cutters. Some of the corporate citrus growers have built company towns out in their groves and the permanent employees live in neat bungalows set around a sandy square.

An estimated 10,000 of Florida's farm workers live in public housing projects that are controlled by the agri-business community. Most of these housing units are taken up by workers who stay in Florida the year round. Those lucky enough to get into one of the better low-rent units pay the rent twelve months a year, even if they do have to follow the crops in the summer.

Historically, these public housing projects have been little better than private housing. Housing authorities in south central Florida for years operated pre-World-War-II migrant camps that had been built by the federal government.

Throughout the farming areas of the nation the Farm Security Administration came to the aid of the migrants in 1939 and 1940, building these temporary 10-by-15-foot shelters at a cost of $100 apiece.

Each shelter contained an electrical outlet and a natural gas outlet. Water, garbage, toilets, and washhouse were all community facilities, shared by the cabin occupants.

After World War II the federal camps were turned over to these public housing authorities. Camps at Pompano, Homestead, Belle Glade, and Pahokee were used to house seasonal farm labor for nearly thirty years. These camps became hellholes, and were finally condemned. Again the agri-business community turned to the federal government for $17 million to replace 1,984 of these tiny shelters.

In an effort to relieve some of the housing shortage, these same housing authorities have borrowed or been granted another $10 million to build new low-income housing. The total $27 million is a federal subsidy to farmers. Even the loans to the public housing authorities can be "excused" if rental incomes do not produce enough revenue to operate the projects and pay off the debt.

In addition to lending or granting funds to the public housing authorities, the U.S. Department of Agriculture, through the Farmers Home Administration, lends low-interest money to farmer cooperatives and to private enterprise for the construction of new farm labor housing. Much of this funding is used to build large, motel-like, two-story apartment structures.

One such structure looked like a large aircraft carrier beached among hundreds of decrepit houses. The big flat-topped building had 100 apartment units and a gross income of approximately $2,000 a week. It had been financed by Farmers Home with a low-interest loan made to a private citizen, an absentee landlord who is in business to make a profit.

Each two-room apartment contained a sink with a cold water faucet, an enclosed bathroom stool and shower, electrical and gas outlets, and nothing else—no heaters, no cupboards, no closets.

When one aging mother of seven asked the landlord for more room, he knocked a hole between two of the apartments, called it a doorway, and doubled her rent. She now pays $120 a month. She can afford electricity to only one of the two apartments. She heats the four 10-by-15-foot rooms with an unvented gas heater, and a tiny two-burner cook stove. This woman's husband is dead; she is partially disabled—one leg was crippled in an accident—and she receives $240 a month in disability benefits and aid to dependent children welfare payments. Each month, after she buys food (she gets food stamps) and pays her utilities, rent, and insurance, she has $15 left. If she and the children didn't do farm work, they could not survive.

As we entered her apartment she insisted we sit on a brand new orange sofa. She sat in a matching chair.

This woman was in her mid-fifties, she had worked all of her life in the fields, and the family had always lived in the small one- and two-room labor camp shanties. There was never enough room. The children had slept three and four to a bed. No one had any privacy.

"This is the first time I've ever had a front room in my house." She smiled, rubbed the plastic covering on the chair, and looked around the room. "Ain't it nice? No one has to sleep in here, ya know."

Now she had space enough for the children to sleep two to a bed—actually two to a mattress on a bare floor—in one bedroom and she shared a bedroom with the smallest child. There was enough room left over for this front room with the couch and chair and a broken TV. In the kitchen she had the small stove, a crooked-legged table and three battered chairs.

I asked her about child labor. Did her own children work?

"Yes sir, they works. Weekends, holidays, like that. I like to keep them in school, but sometimes we jus' can't make it. Then I takes 'em out of school for a day or two, like if it's Friday they work an' then over the weekend and maybe Monday an' that way they gets four days of work, but don't miss but two days of school."

What do the school officials say about this?

"Oh, they know I'm up against it, so they let 'em work some. They understand how it is."

John Kleinert, in the conclusion of his report, commented: "Migrant children attend schools only intermittently and only when it serves an immediate convenience for the family. Most commonly the parents view it as a day care situation freeing them to work the fields without hindrance.

"As soon as the children are old enough to take care of themselves during the day the family pressures on them to ride the school bus decrease. It is not long until the fields claim the migratory young and their meager earnings become a family supplement."

Dr. Robert Coles, a research psychiatrist from Harvard University, who has spent a decade watching, interviewing, and following migrant children up and down the Atlantic Coast, agreed: "By the time these children are 10 or 11 they have had their education, they are no longer children. In many cases, they have stopped going to schools. They are working or helping out with younger children or playing and getting ready to go out on dates and they love and follow in their parents' footsteps. They are to my eye an increasingly sad group of children.

"They have their fun, their outbursts of games and teasing and taunting and laughing; but they are for far too long stretches of time, downcast and tired and bored and indifferent to themselves. They feel worthless, frowned upon and spoken ill of, by the world around them, even by their own parents. Everything seems to brand them and stigmatize them and view them with disfavor . . . the only answer to such a fate is sex, when it becomes available, and drink, when it becomes available."

Dr. Coles, now at work on the fourth volume of *Children of Crisis*, published by Little, Brown, was testifying before Senator Walter Mondale's migratory labor subcommittee.[1] "We see depressions occur about the age of 9 or 10. We see children with severe depressions, a kind of self-destructiveness that knows no bounds. Many of them literally start killing themselves. They take to liquor. They take to violence toward one another or themselves. When a child is 10, he ceases to be a child."

"When a child is 10 he ceases to be a child"—the words have a nightmare quality. Dr. Coles told the senators: "No group of people I have worked with—in the South, in Appalachia, and in our northern ghettos—tries harder to work, indeed travels all over the country, working, working from sunrise to sunset, seven days a week, when the crops are there to be harvested. There is something ironic and special about that, too: in exchange for the desire to work, for the terribly hard work of bending and stooping to harvest our food, these workers are kept apart like no others, denied rights and privileges no others are denied, denied even halfway decent wages, asked to live homeless and vagabond lives . . . ."

There are only 25,000 farm jobs in Florida during the summer. This leaves about 75 percent of the winter migrants jobless at a time when the vegetable and fruit crops in northern states are maturing and ready for harvest. Farmers along the Atlantic Coast and west into Pennsylvania, Ohio, and Michigan are anxious and recruit extensively in Florida. Some of the growers make personal contact with crew leaders, most utilize the interstate services of the federal Rural Manpower Services.

In states like New York and New Jersey farmers place their orders for workers with local RMS offices and these are transmitted to the RMS counterparts in Florida. The manpower officials do not contact workers themselves, but turn these job orders over to crew leaders who recruit the work force needed by the northern farmers.

This recruiting is as casual, as capricious, as avaricious as the daily shapeup in places like Belle Glade's Loading Ramp. This is not to imply that all crew leaders are bad. There are those, like Bob K., who have a reputation as honest men, who treat their workers fairly. Bob acknowledges that some crew leaders do cheat the workers, charging them inflated prices for the necessities of living. "I don't run none of them hustles and none of my row bosses had better either."

Bob is a big man with a deep voice and an easy way of talking with "white folks." He is not an Uncle Tom, nor is he a militant. He's a manipulator, a man who years ago found that his size and his persuasive voice could be used to bridge the gap between the white farmer and the Black worker and that a profit could be turned in the process.

He's a contractor, a businessman who seeks out farmers and offers to harvest their crop at a set price per picking unit, say $1 a basket. He makes the contract in the fall, recruits his crews the following spring—many work for him on a day-haul basis during the winter—and he agrees to pay the workers 75 cents a basket. For the 25 cents he transports, houses, and supervises the crew. Families are provided one-room cabins with cooking privileges—if they bring their own stove. If a worker wants to buy his meals, Bob's wife cooks two meals a day in a central mess hall.

Each spring Bob leaves Florida with 250 workers traveling in five buses and five trucks. Workers who own cars caravan along behind.

"We just travel along slow, it's just like campin' out. There is a government place [rest camp] for migrants in Atlanta, but it is too close. We wouldn't be wore out enough to stop there, so we just go on. When we want to rest, we just pull over."

It sounds much easier than it is. From the Florida Everglades into the eastern half of North Carolina, where Bob's crew first goes to work, is nearly 800 miles. As the caravan leader, Bob knows where he can stop without being run off by a local sheriff. He knows which stores sell food at reasonable prices, which gas stations can furnish parts and repairs for his old trucks and buses.

After three decades of leading workers north, he knows how to move between the white world and the Black workers, between master and slave. Over the years, he has found the best workers to manage are families.

"That's why I been so successful, I taken mostly families. You can get good service out of them family people. Give me the families ever' time.

"We do have a problem in New York, though. Well, we calls it a problem. We have to get workin' permits for every child that is under 16 years of age. That give us quite a bit of a problem because it would be a couple of weeks before the kids could go to work because so many of them is trying to get the permits all at once.

"We take the kids out and let 'em work anyhow and the man, the labor man, comes to the field and he signs up the kids for permits and I get them all in the mail in a big lump sum. The permits is for kids from 10 to 16 years old and the 10-year-olds can only work four hours.

"Now North Carolina don't require no permits for youngsters. But a kid under 10, ain't no use trying to work him, he more trouble to you than he do any good. So we don't try to work any of 'em under 10."

Bob is considering retiring, not because he wants to, but because he sees his profits dwindling. The cost of trucks, gasoline, and food has gone up. The farmers, facing the same increased costs, are turning more and more to machines. But those hand jobs that are left for seasonal farm workers still pay the same low wages. After Bob cuts 25 percent a basket or sack there's too little left. He said, "It's got so the cost of living go to where it just confused everybody's mind . . . they just ain't making it."

A North Carolina blueberry grower, Jason Morris, put it this way: "I have a mechanical harvester that had not been used until we had this problem. I cannot afford to pay more than I have been paying. I paid the maximum. I lost two years in a row. I have gone in the red in the farming operation."

Morris was testifying before the U.S. Senate Subcommittee on Migratory Labor in mid-July of 1969;[2] the problem he referred to was a strike. Most of the 1,000 blueberry pickers had walked out because Morris had refused their demand for a 25-cent increase per 12-pint flat.

These were local workers, recruited from the New Bern area. At least half the crew were children working with their parents. Many of the families had worked on the same farm seasonally for years and they said Morris had not raised the picking price in six years.

Senator Walter Mondale, the committee chairman, asked how long it took an average worker to fill a 12-pint flat. Morris responded: "That is a hard answer to give because we have people from five years old to eighty years old working in my field. I work anybody who comes and wants to pick blueberries.''

Senator Mondale apparently could not believe he had heard the answer correctly: "Five-year-old youngsters?"

Morris: ''Well, he will eat more than he picks, but I will still give him the opportunity to work. Not one man out of a thousand will do what I do.''

Senator Mondale: "You don't have minimum age laws?"

Morris: ''No, we don't say they have got to be 16.''

Senator Mondale: "How long does it take the average worker to pick?"

Morris: ''I will relate a couple of cases. We have a 10-year-old boy who for a season averages $7.50 a day, enough for about an 8- or 9-hour workday.

''We got one lady with four children who on her best day was making $45 a day. She was picking 60 crates of berries per day with her four children less than 15 years old.''

If those examples are computed on a per-worker per-hour basis both the 10-year-old and the woman and her four children were earning $1 an hour or less. The U.S. Department of Agriculture reports the seasonal farm worker in the South Atlantic states earns an average $9 a day for from 139 to 199 days a year. The average seasonal farm worker family income is $2,700 according to these USDA figures.

The problem with these statistics is they average out wild fluctuations and encompass many variable factors. In the Wayne County, New York, cherry and apple harvest, for example, pickers can make as much as $123 a week or as little as $38 a week, depending upon the crop, the time of the season, and the weather. The figures were developed by a state university in a study of migrants over a 17-week period.[3]

The season started off in the cherries at $40 a week and, as the fruit matured, this increased to $86 by the fifth week. As the cherry crop was finished, their wages dropped to an average $38 a week for the next five weeks. During this time there was little work and the harvesters were marking time until the apples ripened. In the last weeks of the apple harvest their wages reach the high point.

By the end of the season the average payroll account showed a total 17-week earnings of $1,122. However, the report warned: "A man and wife and his children will frequently work as a unit. This means that although the payroll records bear only the name of the head of the household, they really reflect the labor and earnings of the total family."

The phenomenon is not unique to New York, or even the East Coast. Anywhere families harvest crops and are paid by the piece rate, the employer—whether labor contractor, crew leader, or grower—is apt to record only a single payroll account and social security number. The families prefer as few deductions as possible and the single-payroll-entry system cuts down the farmer's bookkeeping tasks. It also offers recorded proof that any applicable minimum wage laws are being met and it allows farmers to brag a bit about how much their workers can earn.

Because crew leaders take 10 to 25 percent off the top of the wage structure, many migrants are breaking away and traveling on their own. These "freewheelers" pick their own routes and their own jobs. Where possible, they try to work for small farmers, because their chances of keeping out of a crew-leader system are better. But they don't always succeed.

These workers—and those who come up in crews—expect few niceties while they are on the road. They often live in converted chicken coops, or barns, or old houses. Some of the camps are adequate, a few are even pleasant, but most are bad places to live and to raise children. But the workers know they have little choice, they learn to expect the worst.

Migrant families are resourceful and make do with what they have. If there are no beds, they pull moss out of the trees; if there are no stoves, they dig a pit and cook over an open fire.

Mrs. Ida Brown, a migrant mother of three, explained: "You

know, when you come from Florida, and you come a long ways to get here, you come up here with nothing and you don't expect nothing. Most of the time you scramble around, trying to bum something out . . . ."

We were sitting on the front steps of an old wooden cabin. Her 16-year-old son, Alex, was leaning against the cabin wall, listening. Mrs. Brown talked with her hands as well as her mouth, shaking her finger, slapping her knee to emphasize her words. She and Alex had just come in from the bean fields, their pants were soaking wet because the heavy rains had left the fields wet and muddy. She reported: "The people can't hardly get back to Florida, not this year. Used to be they'd stay up till near through October, but not the way things is this year. We scrimpin' around, trying to find a job. Oh, my goodness, must be two weeks since we worked, on account of the rains.

"We was finishing with the tomatoes, and the rains ended that. Now we just sittin' round here, just hopin' for somebody to come along, give us a day's work."

That day they had been picking beans for $1 a hamper, but there were one hundred people in the field and no one made over $3 or $4 before the field had been picked out. "Well, his beans weren't no good noways. If they'd been any good, he'd a picked 'em with his machines, but because it been rainin' so much, the crop was no good, so he let us pick 'em."

Mrs. Brown is in her late thirties, she has been a migrant most of her life. In addition to Alex, she has two other sons, 12 and 8. Both were enrolled in school in a nearby New Jersey town. She and her husband are separated, and she hopes to make it on her own. She wants to stay in New Jersey, to raise her children there.

She has diabetes, and this causes her problems. But she wants to work: "I like to work, if I can get the full amount. Say they is payin' $1.35 a bushel, and I can go out and earn $1.35 a bushel, yeah, then I want to work. But if I got to buy my own gas, pay my own rent and some crew leader only gives me $1.05 or $1, then I don' wan' it."

She has broken away from the crew leader system by buying her own car and finding her own jobs. She explained: "I know that ol' road just as well any of them crew bosses. We come up in July. The season be off down there in Florida, and we come for the strawberries, then into the beans and tomatoes."

How does the work affect her children?

"It is all right for him," she motioned to the 16-year-old, "but it is too hard on them two younger ones. It really is too hard. I know my little boy, he will say, 'Momma, it's too hot, an' I'm too tired. I ain' gonna do no more.' And he'll go to the car an' go right to sleep. And he is so tired in the mornin' when I go to wake him up, he won' hardly get outta bed.

"Then look at my little boy [the 12-year-old] with the one arm. His other arm was crippled when he was born, and he's not able to be out there pullin' and pickin' but he does it. He picks with the one hand, then he pulls them baskets, then picks some more.

"And sometimes, like this mornin', it is wet out there and you stays wet, because it's rainin', and ever'thin' is wet. My littlest boy, he took down with such a terrible cold, and he was sick . . . ."

Couldn't she leave the younger children in camp?

"No. The reason I wants to take 'em with me is the other children in the camp, they might get into a fight an' so I'd rather have 'em with me, where I can watch 'em."

I asked about pulling and carrying the 30- and 40-pound baskets.

"The way I figure it, that's bad for the children. Say, for instance, you pickin' beans an' you get into some good beans an' you totin' an' the distances [down the row] are long an' as heavy as those hampers is, sometimes you just hurt so bad you gotta crawl out of the field, draggin' 'em behind. You can't even walk, you hurt so bad. The kids shouldn't have to be doin' that from five-thirty or six, whenever the sun comes up, until they can't stand no more.''

Her children do tell her when they get tired, and she lets them rest, or play in the rows. She is proud of her 16-year-old. ''He gets tired, but he won't let you know it. He just wants you to think he's some kind of superman. But I can tell because when [the crew boss] will knock and knock on the door and finally he [her son] will come crawlin' out. And I know he's tired because he can't hardly do the luggin' in the field for me an' him, but he'll do it.''

The two younger children work together in the field, helping each other. Mrs. Brown keeps them in rows close by hers, she coaxes them, teaches them how to pick. In the beans they start out picking one bean at a time, and she gently shows them how to reach in, with both hands, to pull off handfuls before putting the beans in the basket.

Tomatoes are their best crop; on a good day the family can make $18 to $20 at 18 cents a basket. Mrs. Brown got mad as she quoted the prices. The imported workers, the Puerto Rican men brought in by the farmers, were paid 25 cents a basket, but she and her children were getting only 18 cents because they worked for a crew leader. The farmer was paying her crew leader 25 cents; he, in turn, paid his crew 18 cents, taking 7 cents off the top for his ''services.''

As long as she and her children live in the camp the farmer turned over to the crew leader, she must work for that crew leader. For this reason she was searching for a rental house or cabin. ''If you are not livin' on a farm [in a camp] then you have a choice of where you want to work, and you have a chance to leave when you want to. . . .''

She still does not have the freedom she wants because the crew leader system is so strong, but this Black mother is determined. She is not going back to Florida, she is going to settle in New Jersey, she is going to seek welfare assistance, and she is going to continue working.

William Friedland, a professor of community studies at the University of California at Santa Cruz, directed a two-year study of the eastern migrant stream (*Migrant*, Holt, Rinehart and Winston). To gather the material, Friedland sent Cornell University graduate students out into the migrant stream. One of these students, Iles Minoff, was hired into a crew of 62 men, women, and children. The crew worked first in Virginia, then in upstate New York.

There were 12 couples in the crew, two single women with children, 16 single men, and 21 children. They stayed in a farmer's camp, in a compound surrounded by barbed wire. According to Minoff's field notes, there were three rows of one-story cinderblock and wood motel-like structures; each unit was a single, unadorned room. The camp had a communal washhouse, a communal kitchen, and two unmarked privies.

The crew worked primarily in the beans, and were paid daily in tickets. The tickets could be converted to cash at the end of the week, or they could be used to make purchases in a crossroads store where the crew leader had worked out a cooperative agreement with the owner. Because there were no refrigerators in the camp, the crew stopped at the store daily, after work. The families would buy just enough food for their evening meal, a quick cold breakfast, and a lunch.

The prices in the store were only slightly higher than in town, but there was a lot of impulse buying. The children—those over 10, who went into the fields to work—bought ice cream and soda pop and the parents bought a bottle or two of beer; the single men often bought cheap wine or beer.

According to Minoff, the crew worked only four days a week, because Friday was a bad market day for the farmer. During mid-August it rained and the crew worked only two days in two weeks. The rest of the time they lay around camp.

Minoff wrote: "There was nothing to do. After a while, you begin to feel personally contaminated by everything around you." Everything in the camp was either broken or in a state of decay or disrepair; the stench of urine filled the showers, the swampy area back of the camp was stagnant; the men built fires of garbage, refuse, and old tires and then stood in the rain and damp, keeping warm and talking, just to escape the oppressiveness of their tiny rooms.

Minoff observed: "Within the camp it sometimes seemed the children comprised a subculture. Despite the limited physical area of the camp, the children were at times able to define areas for themselves." The youngsters placed great importance on acting grown-up. Sex was often talked about, but there was more joking and teasing than action. The young boys would often tease the girls, telling them they were too young "to give pussy."

The girls would primp and pose and imitate. One 9-year-old, a bright, curious child, acted as a social instructress for the younger girls, showing them how to comb their hair, how to dance and act sexy. The younger children, those below 6, were even further removed from the camp culture. Many of them were bused into a preschool day care center in a nearby town.

Minoff said these younger children were fairly ingenious in their play, creating toys and diversions out of materials at hand. One boy made belts and sashes out of the pull-top beer can lids, then he would drape these over his tiny, black body and parade around the camp proclaiming himself Hercules, the strongest man in the world.

Robert Coles said: "Migrant children begin life as migrants; by and large they are given free rein and begin to crawl. They, of course, do not live in what we would call houses, but in cabins, and they do considerable running about. I might say that when they are 7 or 8, some of them begin working. They are active children. They move around a lot. They are not afraid of being with one another and they huddle together as poor children huddled together in the nineteenth century.

"Migrant children by the thousands not only live in poverty, go hungry, suffer from malnutrition, but in addition live incredibly uprooted lives . . . these children eventually become dazed, listless, numb to anything but immediate survival. From birth on for such children, it is travel and all that goes with travel. That is forced travel, undertaken by migrant farm workers who roam the American land in search of crops to harvest and enough dollars to stay alive."

Coles carries a drawing board, pencils, and crayons and he frequently asks a child to draw pictures for him. As they draw, they explain what it is they are expressing. Tom, a seven-year-old, drew a rather dreary picture of the fields he already knew as a helper to his parents.

Coles explained: "This seven-year-old boy is a harvester, really, because he was five when I first saw him walking down those rows of beans, picking. Sometimes he would show his age by pointing out achievements, by pointing out to anyone near at hand how much he had done, how experienced he had become. Children are often like that, a little enthusiastic and a little boastful."

Commenting on Tom's picture of the fenced field, guarded by faceless men, Coles said: "I think this child has already seen himself somewhat hemmed in, and imprisoned, not only by the arrangements in the field, but by the whole way of life that is his."[4]

4

It takes a great deal of patience just to tolerate some children where work is being done. Frankly we would not allow them in our orchards if we did not feel a responsibility to our local community. Children are not efficient workers.

—*A Pennsylvania farmer*

Los Trabajadores

"We knew everything about cotton, the planting, the thinning, the chopping, and the picking. We were eight in our family, counting my mother and father, and we had this old truck. We stayed with the cotton, and we never left Texas. We didn't travel far, not like now.

"The cotton was our life. I would really get on top of a row of cotton, man, because I was a damn good picker. I was only 12 or 13 years old, but I could pull! I could pull 900 pounds. The only other ones that could do that were 23 or 24 years old. Not even my own father, who was a strong man, could beat me. It was a skill when you weigh only 80 or 90 pounds to pull the 120 pounds in the cotton sack.

"We used to get up early and wait for the sun. If you pick when the dew is on the cotton it's wet and weighs more. In the field there was always a race with somebody. It was a challenge, you know? Sometimes you'd hear about a good picker from another gin and you'd want to make sure he heard about you.

"We were making $2 a hundred when the machines came. Oh, we'd heard about them for quite a while before we saw one, but we couldn't figure how in the hell a machine could pick without getting the green leaves, the pears [unopened bolls], the clods, and the snakes all mixed up with the cotton. But it did, and then they began to let us work the ends, where the machines turned around, and they paid us $2.15 but there were too many people and there wasn't that much work."

Narcisio was 14 when the machines rumbled into the cotton fields his family had worked. The mechanical pickers were an inventor's nightmare, ugly, giant red bugs with great screen cages high up on their backs. Down low, in front, was the awful mouth, where hundreds of barbed spindles whirled on two counter-rotating drums. The spindles pulled the cotton from the bolls and a vacuum sucked it up into the big screen cage on top.

Narcisio, now 22, recalled, "I lost a great deal when that machine came into the field." The words are nostalgic and slightly bitter, the proper reminiscence of a man twice his age. His father heard there was a need for tomato pickers in Florida. They packed up the truck and moved to Immokalee.

Narcisio remembers: "When we started in the tomatoes, all I could do was trip over the vines, but after a while I could do pretty good. Tomatoes were a good crop, but we had to move around a lot."

The family became interstate migrants, traveling through South Carolina, Pennsylvania, and Ohio, returning each winter to Texas for a few weeks before going back to Florida. Cotton-picking was only a memory, something to brag about.

The National Cotton Council reported that 98 percent of the cotton crop is now picked by machines; 95,000 mechanical pickers and mechanical strippers have eliminated 1,400,000 jobs. From the Deep South, through Texas and Oklahoma, into the southwest and on to California the cotton crop once carried hundreds of thousands of workers from early spring chopping and thinning through the fall and winter picking. While there still is some hand chopping and thinning work left, the nation's cotton is now harvested by 95,000 machine operators and their 45,000 helpers.

For years a man bent over the cotton row, dragging the long, white cotton sack, symbolized the migrant farm worker, and the shanty cotton camps were evidence of the migrants' misery. In the mid-1930's a social scientist, Paul Taylor, noted: "Many of those going into the cotton fields of Texas are accompanied by their entire families. This is to the liking of the planters for it is maintained that the children, as a rule, will pick as much cotton as the grownups."

In the Oklahoma Dust Bowl entire families of white yeoman farmers were driven from the land by the wind and the tractors of large landholders. These small farmers became the California cotton pickers, the Okies who competed with the Mexican families coming north from Tijuana and Mexicali, Juarez and Reynosa.

South of the border there was an inexhaustible supply of cheap labor: Los Mojados (the wetbacks), Los Braceros (the strong-armed contract workers), and the Green Card (legal) aliens who crossed the border for a day, a week, a year to work on the farms. The pressure of these workers coming across the border makes the lower Rio Grande Valley of Texas the wellspring of the migrant stream. No other place has supplied more seasonal labor to the farm states of this nation.

A 1938 study of 300 Mexican families from South Texas showed most worked in the winter vegetables through March and then headed north. Some stopped to work the onions, but 60 percent traveled on into Michigan and Montana and Colorado to thin and weed the sugar beets. The work was a family affair, the labor of the children was vital to the family income.

Now an estimated 80,000 to 90,000 workers and their families migrate out of the Rio Grande Valley each year; they spend from five to nine months following the crops into Florida or

Pennsylvania or Indiana. They travel into the Pacific Northwest and into California. No corner of the nation escapes their search for work.[1]

Each year some try to settle out. There are thousands of Mexican-American farm worker families living in California, Colorado, Michigan, Ohio, New Jersey, and Florida. Most of them will tell you they are from Texas. They still claim the cities and the rural colonias of "El Valle" as their true homes.

El Valle—the abbreviated name the migrants have given the Rio Grande Valley—is an immense, fertile, flat land, in the southernmost part of Texas, a four-county area watered by the Rio Grande River as it curves east toward the Gulf of Mexico. Farmers there grow $100 million worth of citrus, winter vegetables, and melons.

Nearly 400,000 people live in the valley; two-thirds of them have Spanish surnames, most are Mexican-American farm workers, second- and third- and fourth-generation citizens who have or are attempting to establish homes in the urban barrios and the rural colonias.

There are 200 of these remote colonias dotting the flat south Texas landscape. Most are dirt road subdivisions where the poor can buy small lots for a few hundred dollars and begin to put together a home. These families feel the need to own a piece of land, they want some place to put down roots.

The land is important. To protect it, a family will buy a strong fence, often going deeper in debt to buy the strongest, most expensive chain link fencing available. Throughout these colonias empty lots are guarded by such fences while the families are off traveling, seeking work to pay off the debts and start a home.

For the Sanchez family, home is a two-cabin affair that has been completely renovated. Mrs. Sanchez explained, "We first bought an old cabin for $250 and had it moved here. It was this one."

She motioned around the building we were in. It contained a living room where we sat, a kitchen and dining area, and a small area for Mrs. Sanchez' washing machine and dryer. In the wall above the dining area a hole had been cut and a new air conditioner had been installed.

"My 16-year-old son purchased that for me when we got back from Utah. He and my oldest daughter bought some paint and painted all the inside. I wanted them to save their money for school, and I know we should have used the money for something beside that air conditioner, but he wanted so much to make it nice in here, I couldn't disappoint him."

The Sanchez family purchased its second used cabin after the first had been paid for and remodeled. This second unit was divided into bedrooms for Mr. and Mrs. Sanchez and their seven children. This building is smaller and it is crowded, but if they have another season as good as the last, Mrs. Sanchez said they will make an addition.

The family has been traveling north, into Indiana and Illinois to harvest tomatoes, into Utah to hoe and thin sugar beets. They leave when school is out and try to make it back within two or three weeks of the time school starts again. They travel in their own cars—they need two—and find their own jobs.

"We don't go with the contractors anymore because we don't like to be rented out like that. We are human beings, not animals to be rented." The only time I detected any hostility in this gentle woman was when she made this statement. The emotion quickly disappeared.

She and the children travel and work each summer while Mr. Sanchez stays behind to work at a full-time farm job. Even a steady job is subject to the weather and cropping patterns. Workers coming across the border keep the wages low. Without the work of the children, the family could hardly survive. Most of the families living in this colonia depend upon making enough in the north to carry them through the winter.

The parents may find a few days of work each month; sometimes they will take the older children out of school to work if something opens up. But there are days and weeks on end when there is no work. During this time the families work on their homes, making an addition, drilling a well, digging a pit toilet.

Winters in south Texas can be economic disasters if a hurricane strikes the Gulf Coast or there are unseasonal rains. The political climate is extremely conservative. County governments are controlled by the farm interests and their city agribusiness partners. Welfare is dispensed grudgingly, and then usually in the form of USDA surplus commodities. A month's supply lasts barely two weeks.

By spring the families are broke and desperate for work. In early April some begin to board up their homes, padlock the gates, and head out on the seven-month trek in search of work. It's ironic that as they leave, the spring work in Texas is beginning. But winter through summer most of those jobs go to the men, women, and children coming across the border.

In 1940 the Mexican population along the United States–Mexican border was 2.6 million. In 1970 it was estimated at 8 million.[2] Across from Brownsville (51,000 population) there is La Ciudad de Matamoros with 143,000 people and across from McAllen (36,000) there is Reynosa with 134,000 people.[3]

Mexicans who can earn only 3,270 pesos ($261) a year in the interior of Mexico come north to the border searching for higher-paying jobs and a chance to enter the United States legally or illegally to work. If a family of five can secure papers, or can bluff or sneak their way across the international bridges that link the American and Mexican cities, their incomes soar to $2,000 or $3,000 a year.

A U.S. Labor Department investigator wrote: "It was four in the morning, chilly for March in Brownsville [Texas] and the workers from Mexico straggled across the bridge in twos and threes, braced for their daily confrontation with the United States Government.

"These were farm workers. There were men and women and boys and girls, all Mexican, all poor, all headed to nearby street corners where local farmers hired them on the spot and then loaded them onto flatbed trucks for the trip to the farm, maybe forty miles away.

"Many of the workers were fourteen and fifteen; they had been born in America and showed the man at the bridge their battered birth and baptismal certificates. The Fair Labor Standards Act makes it illegal to employ a child under 16 while school is in session and Brownsville schools would be opening a few hours later.

"Normally it is hard to enforce child labor in agriculture—warning whistles send the smaller kids out of the fields while the bigger ones simply lie. Here, at the farm workers' shapeup, where the youngsters had to carry a birth certificate, was a made-to-order enforcement situation. But nobody cared."

The investigator David North, reported: "The fact the unemployment is high and the wage rates are low in the border towns is not coincidental. An estimated 100,000 workers residing in Mexico contribute to the labor surpluses by filling jobs that American residents would otherwise have—and frequently take them at wage rates unacceptable to United States residents."[4]

Effect?

In the Brownsville–Harlingen–San Benito area of Texas, family incomes average $3,216 a year, the second lowest in the nation.

Thousands of the border crossers are U.S. citizens who have never lived in the United States. For years pregnant mothers from Matamoros and Reynosa have come across the border to have their children here. These children are U.S. citizens and when they are 10 or 12 they begin to come across the border to work in the fields of the lower Rio Grande.

They come across in the dark before dawn and go to where the labor contractors' trucks and buses are lined up. They hope to get a job, to make $5 or maybe $10. They are willing to ride two or three or even four hours on the buses because the farther north they go the higher the pay.

Like all other workers in these shape-ups, they compete for a seat on the bus. They compete for work. The crew leaders contract with the growers either on a flat per-acre fee or on a piece rate. Either way, the crew leader takes 10 to 20 percent off the top and hires the workers. Some unscrupulous crew leaders also require a kickback of from $5 to $20 a week.

For such a "consideration" the worker is guaranteed a bus seat and more hours of work. A Mexican boy in his late teens explained, "If you can make $40 or $50 a week it is better to give the contractor $10 or $15 than not to work at all, or to stay in Mexico and try to find a job at $1 or $2 a day."

These two forces—workers who cross the border and mechanization—are pervasive. The farm workers who live in the valley have no defense. They were cotton pickers before the machines came; their lives—no matter how poor—had some predictability.

Children like Narcisio learned to hoe and to pick almost as soon as they could walk. They went to the fields with their parents, they would play in the rows, they would sleep in the cars or in the shade of the truck, but they also learned the work as they picked into their mothers' cotton sacks. They were taught how to reach into the cotton boll with their fingers, to pull and wad the cotton until they had a handful, they were taught to alternate left and right hand, to set a pace. Their tiny fingers bled, then toughened and became calloused to the rasping edges of the open cotton bolls.

But by the age of 14 Narcisio was replaced by a machine. What he had learned was no longer useful. Now he is 22 and a skilled tomato picker, but machines are coming into that crop.

Machines now harvest wine grapes, walnuts, corn, prunes,

olives, and almonds; even fresh peaches are being experimentally machine-picked, and it will not be long before there are mechanical citrus harvesters.

Without these labor-saving advances in technology many farmers would go broke; mechanized harvesting reduces the peak seasonal labor demand. Because this levels and stabilizes the farmer's needs, it sounds desirable. It is—for the farmer and for those few farm workers who convert to mechanized jobs.

However, as the number of jobs decreases, the number of Mexican alien workers coming through the border, legally and illegally, does not diminish. Competition for jobs gets more intense. Wages remain low.

When the crop is mechanized, the hand-labor force scatters. Families seek other jobs in other crops. Some manage to escape farm labor altogether. Many find so little work they must seek help from welfare. The impact of mechanization on the existing labor pool is quite like hitting a blob of mercury with a hammer.

In theory the federally funded $23 million-a-year Rural Manpower Service operating in 38 states is supposed to help workers find jobs. However, the Service, created by the 1933 Wagner-Peyser Act to aid farm labor, is so dominated by farmers that farm workers use it only as a last resort.

An example of RMS service was described in a suit filed against the RMS by the California Rural Legal Assistance on behalf of 250 farm workers. In an affidavit, one worker told of being hired through the RMS office in Calexico: "When we arrived in Washington, we found that the camp was crowded with people. As our bus from California was pulling in, buses were arriving from El Paso, Texas, and Nogales, Arizona. There were at least 500 people in the camp at that time.

"Unfortunately there was not enough work for all of us. We were allowed to work only two to three hours per day . . . the work prospects were so bad that many of the people began leaving the camp. After I got back to Calexico, I saw the state farm labor placement office still had its sign posted asking people to go to work for the Green Giant in Washington.''

Rather than experience such problems, workers seek out jobs on their own, either through labor contractors and crew leaders, or through the grapevine that operates wherever seasonal farm workers migrate. Workers hear ''you can make it pretty good'' in Washington apples, or California grapes; they learn that potatoes in Maine are picked by the school kids. Somebody has an uncle in Oregon who will know where work is to be found, or there is a cousin in the San Juan Valley in Colorado who is fixed pretty well. Maybe there is something there.

The family loads up the truck, a cousin brings some of the kids with him in a car, and they are off.

In the late 1950's and early 1960's Texas cotton pickers put out of work by the machines found they could plant tomatoes in Ohio in the early spring, go to Michigan for the cherry harvest, and then return to Ohio in mid-August for the tomato harvest.

Ohio wanted the migrants to come into the state and went to considerable effort to get them to return each year. Job orders were placed through the RMS. Farmers would recruit families on their own, writing or telephoning to Texas to urge good workers to come back.

Annually from 30,000 to 35,000 migrants moved into the Ohio tomato crop; most were family workers from Texas. Ohio build an elaborate central receiving center for the families. Centrally located in Henry County, it contained a rest camp, playgrounds with swings and sand boxes, a laundromat, a television, ping-pong tables and shuffle board courts.

It had a health center and job information center. When the facility opened in 1965 one official commented: ''This state has a certain obligation to see that the migrant group is afforded reasonable comfort and advantages while passing through or temporarily residing here. It is important that Ohio present a fair and friendly countenance to these wayfarers upon whom we depend so much.''[5]

During the late 1960's these recruiting efforts were successful. Reverend Albert H. Ottenweller, speaking for the governor's committee on migratory labor, proclaimed the 1967 migrant season "the most successful in the history of Ohio, with perhaps the largest production of all time both in total acres and in yield per acre."

What the Reverend did not mention was that a very large part of the successful harvest was gathered in by child labor. While Ohio has fairly elaborate child labor laws, neither these nor the federal Fair Labor Standards Act have prevented what one federal official finally labeled "a very ugly situation."

In 1970 the American Friends Service Committee field teams observed entire families—including children as young as six —working in the pickle (cucumbers) fields and in the sugar beets. In the pickles the AFSC reported: "Each family is assigned a section [of the field] and they get half the crop from that section." Thus the parents, not the farmer or the labor crew leader, are the employers of the children. This tactic circumvents federal and state child labor laws.

A more dramatic measure of child labor has occurred yearly in the tomato harvest in the northwest quarter of the state. Ohio brags about its $135 million tomato crop; the state ranks first in the production of tomato juice and second in canned tomatoes, catsup, and puree.

For the four years ending with the 1970 season, it also had the dubious distinction of leading the nation in violations of the federal FLSA proscriptions against the employment of children under 16 years of age while school was in session. The tomato harvest in these 17 counties starts in mid-August and lasts through mid-October.

When school starts in September eight federal wage and hour inspectors go into the fields. In only six days in 1969 they found 364 children working. In 1970 the count totaled 340 children found working on 77 farms in the 17 counties. Of these, 75 were between the ages of 6 and 9 and another 123 were between 10 and 12.

Most of the Ohio tomato growers are small family farmers. They will grow corn, some wheat or oats or soybeans, and 20 to 30 acres of tomatoes. Some will have a livestock sideline, usually swine. A 320-acre farm would be large. These farmers and their own children do most of the labor. But in the spring each grower hires tomato workers himself or contracts with a crew leader for a specific number of workers. A rule of thumb: one worker can handle two acres.

Liberty Center farmer Walter Bostleman plants 27 to 35 acres of tomatoes a year and hires 15 to 20 people. "Right now I got an awful good bunch, two families, awful nice people. They could eat in my house at my table, that's how clean and dependable they are. They come from Texas, and they are not as rough on the vines. My grade is a lot better. Those other people [the crew he had last year] could pick more tomatoes, but when they got ahold of something, they wouldn't let loose [they bruised the fruit]."

The pickers go over a field four times, picking the red ripe tomatoes. Bostleman pays 16 cents a 33-pound hamper. The two families Bostleman hired are composed of four adults and 22 children, a fact that caused Bostleman to laugh and comment, "You can see they don't just pick tomatoes."

Bostleman houses the families on his farm. "We had an old chicken coop that I converted into a house, then I had two other houses moved in. I set them up like I thought I was supposed to [by law], but I give that up because they [the families] will arrange it like they want it. These two families even put plywood in there [the chicken coop] for privacy, they boarded up the door between the families."

Bostleman said he urges the parents to send the youngest children to school. Instead the parents bring all the children to the tomato fields. He has told the parents to keep the children from working "but they duck in when I go to haul the tomatoes to the plant. I haul my own tomatoes, and I'm gone from one to two hours. The kids work when I'm out of the field. This one time when I got back there sat the federal man. No use for me to lie to him."

Other Ohio farmers with whom I talked had also been cited for illegal use of child labor—and also claimed the parents wanted the children to work. One put it this way: "They don't haul those 13- and 14-year-olds around for nothing, some of 'em are as big as their fathers and can pick like any adult."

Many of the parents admit keeping their children out of school. They say the month or six weeks spent in the Ohio schools is not counted by Texas school officials.

A Florida migrant mother complained the Ohio school officials put her children back a grade when they entered school in September, so she kept them out to work. She said, "They work from the time the sun comes up until 8:30 [a.m.] when the school bus comes by. Then they don't stay in the field, but when it's time for the children to be home from school, they [her six school-age children] come back out in the field to work."

Some of the parents send their children to school and work them after they return in midafternoon. A farmer explained, "By afternoon the parents are gettin' tired; those hampers weigh 30 or 35 pounds, so after lunch they'll fill 'em and just let them set in the rows until the kids get home from school. Then they come out in the field and haul the hampers for their parents."

Richard Detling of Union City is one of the largest tomato growers in the state; in the late 1960's he was also a member of the Ohio Governor's Committee on Migrant Labor. Federal wage and hour agents cited him, alleging he worked children under 16 while school was in session. The citation was a civil complaint.

Detling was contesting the allegation and therefore could

not talk about his specific case. However, he answered general questions.

Why the crackdown in Ohio?

"Well, they are just more aggressive in enforcing the laws that have been on the books for 30 years."

What was the cause of the child labor problem?

"As far as the Mexican families are concerned," Detling said, "they want the children to work and they need them to work. Of course [the children] represent a source of income for the family."

Then, without being asked about welfare, Detling said, "As long as we have hand harvest of the tomato crop, we will need the migrants because the locals won't do the job. These local workers can be out of work and have no prospects in sight and they won't pick tomatoes, they won't do any kind of stoop labor."

Why?

"Just because it isn't necessary. If a person doesn't want to work—in Ohio it is just like it is everywhere else—they don't have to work because the welfare will take care of them."

There are local farm workers in Ohio, just as there are in every farming area. There are also unemployed workers in nearby towns and cities who could come out and work on the farms if the pay was higher.

Stoop labor averages at best $10 or $15 a day, if the crop is good, if it isn't raining, and if there aren't too many workers in the field. A man might make $50 to $75 a week, but the season is too short and the working conditions are too uncertain to be attractive to local workers, so migrants are recruited.

The great irony, of course, is that the migrants who come to Ohio to pick tomatoes are the local workers of the Rio Grande Valley. Their jobs in the cotton were taken over by machines. If they stay in Texas they must compete with border-crossing aliens who are willing to work for only $5 or $10 a day. The pay is not enough, so they come north.

But now they face a new threat from machinery. The cherry harvests in Michigan are being mechanized. These migrants must find other work to fill the weeks between the tomato planting and harvest times. But even if they do, it is only a matter of time before the tomato harvest is fully mechanized in Ohio.

One Ohio tomato grower explained why the mechanization of tomatoes has been so slow: "We can't afford to own one of those [$25,000] machines and when you get three or four farmers together, you know what happens. They can't agree on anything. One will want to harvest today, but the other has his crop ready, too.

"The last two or three years, we seen three or four machines at work. Last year my brother-in-law contracted to have one come in, but there was a mix-up. The machine went somewhere else and didn't show up for a week. All the fruit he lost was disgraceful; he got only 20 tons out of a 30-ton crop. I told him I'd have found me 30 laboring people instead, that's what I'd have done."

The USDA estimates mechanization and the development of new herbicides and other chemical and technological advances eliminate 22,000 seasonal farm labor jobs a year. Much of this "progress" is financed by federal and state funds.

Each year the USDA spends $400 million on its own research and development programs, on grants to the state colleges and universities conducting agricultural research, on the agriculture extension service, the farm advisors who aid the farmer, and on the USDA extension research stations. For instance, engineers at the University of California at Riverside–USDA cooperative experiment station have spent eight years and nearly $1 million trying to develop a mechanical citrus harvester. Two-thirds of the funds have come from the USDA.

Private industry in California and Florida has spent similar amounts trying to mechanize the citrus harvest. Finally, a syndicate of three private companies, utilizing technology developed by the USDA in Michigan—for mechanical cherry pickers —and California, has come up with a mechanical orange picker that may prove commercially acceptable.

A USDA agriculture research engineer explained that such federally developed technology is in the "public domain" and available for use by anyone, private industry included. Some of the state college systems retain the patents and charge industry for the use of their ideas. The federal government does not.

Congress asked USDA officials what was being done to aid the farm workers who were displaced by the federally subsidized mechanization of farming. One bureaucrat admitted: "There has been more enthusiasm on the part of the appropriation agencies to support research work in production efficiency than there has been to support research work in the areas of migrant labor."

How much was the USDA seeking to begin to rectify this oversight, to begin researching the needs of displaced workers? $100,000.

What would the money be used for?

A USDA economist replied: "We will try to count them [migrants] better. In addition we need to know a lot more about where migrants live, where they start from, how they find out where their work patterns are, what their opportunities are as the migrant stream continues to dwindle."

The USDA knows little or nothing about people like Narcisio, or Jimmy Brooks, or Ida Brown; the Department's statisticians estimate there are 257,000 migrants, but they admit there may be a 22 percent error in their statistical computations and there is no accounting for child labor.[6]

Each year the migrant statistics published by the USDA drop and this reduction is the proof that agriculture's ostrichlike position is working. If the migrant situation is ignored the machines will eventually solve the problem by eliminating the hand labor; if the USDA speeds up the mechanization process, the migrant problem will disappear faster.

The American Farm Bureau Federation—the voice of two million farm families—puts a little different emphasis on the issue of worker versus machine. I asked Matt Triggs, the AFBF senior lobbyist, what responsibility the farmer had to the worker who is replaced by a machine.

Triggs: "Farmers are reacting against an impossible situation in their determined efforts to reduce their dependence upon a labor force—and they are dependent upon a labor force.

"Farmers, in their own self-interest, have got to find ways and means of doing things more efficiently and that means utilizing fewer workers. . . . They have reduced farm labor by 1.9 million in the past 9 years . . . [and] there are other things they can do and will do if the general society insists on creating conditions that make it impossible for them to employ workers on an acceptable basis. . . ."

Triggs seemed to be saying that society—by enacting minimum wage, child labor, and other worker protection laws —was imposing impossible conditions on the farmer. The AFBF for 35 years has opposed such laws for farm workers. Its position, as expressed by Triggs, is that there is a "general societal responsibility" for displaced workers but that the farmer does not share in that responsibility.

Triggs: "You gotta keep in mind that the farmer's gotta make a living, too, and a lot of them are on the ragged edge, a lot of them are close to bankruptcy."

There is no doubt that the cost of labor is one of the most troubling economic factors faced by the farmer. He needs large numbers of workers for relatively short periods; in statistical terms his account records show these workers are one of the largest cash drains on his business.

But mechanization does not solve the "migrant problem." Some workers will successfully convert to the more mechanized farm labor force, but there will be only enough work for a relatively small number. It is argued that those who find machine jobs will be better off because mechanization means higher skills and higher pay. That is not always true. Teen-age boys are driving cotton-picking machines in the Rio Grande Valley for $1.25 to $1.50 an hour, and if they don't like the pay, they can climb down and let someone else have the job.

One cotton industry official laughingly told how south Texas cotton growers combined the threat of mechanization with the overabundant supply of labor to keep picking costs down: They parked the machines beside the fields and told the hand pickers the wage was $2 a hundred, take it or leave it. The average worker could make $5 to $7 a day. If they complained, the machines would finish the harvest.

Antonio Orendain, a farm worker turned farm labor organizer in the Rio Grande Valley, commented: "With the machines they say you can make more if you drive, but it is not true. In 1951, when I was still illegal [he was an illegal alien for five years], we did not hear of the machines. I picked cotton for $3 or $3.50 [a hundredweight]. They were paying more then than at the present time. Then later, when I was legal, I got a job driving a cotton picking machine. Then I made $2 an hour, but now, because of the competition at the border, to drive the machines the farmers only pay $1.20 or $1.25 an hour. I could make more picking cotton by hand twenty years ago."

Orendain is the director of the United Farm Workers Union in Texas. As part of that union effort, he has an early morning, Spanish-language radio show that penetrates deep into Mexico. Called "Voice of the Farm Worker," it is used to counter grower radio-recruiting efforts.

Orendain claims the growers' radio spots call for more workers than are needed. "Maybe the radio asks for 100 workers for Mississippi or Minneapolis. They put the radio spot on every 30 minutes. Just think of how many people across in Mexico hear this and try to come. That is why the growers end up with 200 workers when maybe they only need 50.''

When the union ''makes'' a strike anywhere, in Texas or California or Ohio, strikebreakers are recruited from the Rio Grande Valley or from Mexico. Orendain explained: ''We realized that we had to go into Mexico and organize the workers there, too. They are the ones that come through to work on the farms here.''

In addition to strikebreaking pressures, these commuting alien workers cause other problems. Orendain says: ''There are many children 8 and 10 years old coming through, whole families come in to this country to work. And these women and kids take away the work of men. They [the growers] say it is a beautiful thing, you take your kid with you to work, and the kid learns to earn his daily bread. Or they tell you take your kids to the day care center, and then your wife will not have to worry while she works.''

Orendain asked, ''How do you think it makes me feel to have to have my wife and my children work because I cannot make enough for them to live? It is one thing if a wife helps her husband so the family can have a better place and better living. It is something else if the man cannot make enough to feed his family without them working, too.

''Most of the families from the valley, they have to go wherever they can find the work. The ones that used to come to California to break the grape strike [Delano, 1965] used to make us mad, but we knew they had to have the money. They would tell us how bad things were for them back here in the valley. Most of them were making a home here, they would have a lot and their house.''

Ricardo and Juan are the sons of a Texas migrant family that has settled out in the Willamette Valley of Oregon. Both were attending a university in the Pacific Northwest. They were four years out of the migrant life, but they had not forgotten it.

Ricardo said: "I can remember when I went to the army, I couldn't get over how much I was being paid. I really felt guilty, you know. But the money is why you see so many Chicano guys in the service. It's so goddamn much better than what you had."

It was Sunday and the boys were home from college. All of the family was gathered in their parents' home. Someone mentioned that a neighboring family, former migrants from Texas like themselves, had packed up and left the Willamette Valley the week before. They were going to try to settle in southern Idaho.

Juan explained that migrant families like theirs had come to Willamette and found there was vine work and planting in the spring, that there were early summer strawberries to be picked and then a large bean crop that lasted into the fall. During the winter a man could pick up extra work and the children could go to school. The best-paying crop for the workers was strawberries; a good picker could make 30 crates a day and was paid 70 to 80 cents a crate. It was a crop the whole family would work well in. The word spread across the migrant routes: the Willamette was a good place to settle.

Juan's father said, "When we came to this valley in 1967, we were paid 3 cents a pound in the beans and if you worked hard you could make 700 pounds in a long day. Now there is still some hand-picking, the machines haven't taken it all; but there are too many pickers in the fields. A worker is lucky if he can make 400 pounds before the field is finished. We don't work much past noon because the field is picked out."

Juan picked up the conversation again. "Because of the machines and the large numbers of people showing up in the fields, some families are taking off. Some are going up into Washington into the apples, some are headed into California.

This family we speak of is trying Idaho. What they are doing is running from the machines, trying to find a place where they can work and earn enough to live.''

Ricardo and Juan and I went outside for a while, to sit under an old shade tree and talk. It was obvious both had strong feelings for the Rio Grande Valley and their home town, San Juan, but they had no love for the migrant life.

''We would drive day and night, day and night, you know?'' Ricardo said, ''I was little then, but I remember I would get up next to the back wall. [Their father had built a wooden camper to protect those riding in back.] I would look down between the wall and the back and I could see the white line going past. I would watch it until I got dizzy. Sometimes I would get sick, but mostly it would put me to sleep. You were always going. You never belonged anyplace. You are driving and the people are looking funny at you, as you go by.''

David, a 17-year-old friend who lived nearby, had come up and was listening. He said, ''Sometimes you gotta stop, you get so tired. You park on a side road somewhere and you rest, but you don't stay long, because you don't want to get in trouble. Sometimes the cops run you off, tell you get the hell away. It's not very easy to travel from here to there, sometimes you feel the prejudice. They won't let you in a restaurant or they chase you off from the bathroom at the gas station.''

Juan cut in, ''It is real bad in Texas. The Anglos looked down on you. Maybe when they were little kids, they would play with you, but not when they got older.''

Were they treated badly in the farm towns in the north?

''Sometimes, but most of the Americans are friendly.'' David used the word American to refer to local townspeople and Mexican to refer to himself and the other workers. He said on the Fourth of July in the small Wisconsin town near where they worked, the ''Americans'' played baseball against the ''Mexicans.''

Ricardo said, ''In the North, like in Ohio, where we were,

we'd be on the farm, staying on the farm, and the atmosphere was different. The Anglos would intermingle with you and there was this feeling that although you were different, you were wanted.''

David's father had been injured in a fall from a trailer. He had broken some ribs and injured his back seriously. The family was without funds and farm workers were without any kind of medical insurance or workman's compensation, so the injuries were never treated properly and the father's ability to work and to move around grew progressively more painful. He can no longer work.

David assumed leadership in the family when he was fourteen. During the migrant season David's father remained in Texas while the rest of the family traveled north to work in the sugar beets. Although he had no driver's license, David was the oldest, and the only one besides his father who could drive. The boy took the family north successfully for two seasons before moving to Oregon.

They, like thousands of other families, got their sugar beet job assignments from a huge corporation that recruited extensively throughout south Texas during the winter. Most of these sugar companies give workers a small stipend—a cent or two a mile for each worker over 14 years old—to get to the job in Minnesota or Utah or Colorado. Sugar beets are grown extensively throughout the Midwest and West.

Under special federal regulations covering the production of sugar, workers must be 14 years old, and must receive a minimum hourly wage—now $1.85 an hour—or a specific piece rate per acre that in theory works out to be the guaranteed hourly minimum for an "average" worker.

Sugar companies tend to recruit more workers than are needed. One worker who had driven 1,500 miles reported: "We arrived [at Bayard, Nebraska] at 2:30 p.m. There were three or four families already there waiting to be assigned to a grower. One family from Weslaco [Texas] had been waiting since Wednesday [three days] and about an hour after we had arrived, a man who I presume was a grower, came and took them.

"The general manager came and we introduced ourselves. He said he was very sorry, but that he had bad news for us, that he thought he could not find us housing. He told us we were not the only ones he was turning back to Texas."

While the company policies vary, workers in the beets in Minnesota and Michigan reported the companies "loaned" the workers $45 or $50 a week for living expenses and wages were withheld until the end of the season. The families would contract with the company for a specific acreage, agreeing to go over each acre twice, thinning and blocking the field with short-handled hoes. The workers were assigned housing, usually rent-free. Sometimes these labor camps were decent, sometimes they were shanty camps with foul pit privies, dirty showers, and washrooms.

One 16-year-old boy, who had been working in the beets since he was 11, told of how a farmer, five years before, had given the family a trailer to use each year. Each season, as the family grew, the trailer deteriorated, and living conditions became worse, but the farmer failed to make repairs. The toilet did not work, the roof leaked, three of the boys had to sleep on the floor of the trailer because there wasn't enough room for more beds. Despite the bad housing conditions, this family returned to the same farm year after year because the farmer treated them fairly, his farming practices made the work more tolerable, and his pay was above average.

When farmers recruit workers during the winter, they have no accurate way to set a starting date. Crop maturity depends on the weather, but the workers must be there when the crop is ready and so the tendency is to set the date a bit early. In Colorado in 1967 workers recruited for the cucumber crop arrived to find work wouldn't start for two or three weeks. Rains had delayed the crop. The sugar beet season was just coming to an end, but there were a few fields left to hoe.

Jonathan B. Chase, a University of Colorado professor of law and a director of the Colorado Rural Legal Services, was spending the summer as a beet worker.[7] He reported that labor contractors were giving the cucumber workers jobs in the beet fields but were paying only 50 cents to 60 cents a row. The workers could only make 30 to 40 cents an hour because the rows were long and weedy.

Chase was on a crew that had been told by the contractor that the farmer was paying only 60 cents a row and giving the contractor $1 an acre for supervising the 36 acres of work. Later, Chase interviewed the grower and found that he had actually paid the contractor $2 an acre, and $1 a row. While the families were receiving less than the federally guaranteed wages or piece rate, the contractor in two days time made a $240 profit, more than the grower's net return on the crop.

These workers were mostly Texas migrant families. While the law prohibits workers under 14 in the sugar beet fields, many of the families work their younger children, just as they do in other crops.

And here, too, the families are threatened with mechanization. A USDA official, in a letter to Senator Mondale, stated that new herbicides and new electronically operated mechanical weeders had already replaced 10,000 sugar beet and cotton thinning and weeding jobs throughout the United States.

5

It don't hurt kids to pick a few peppers out there, or a few grapes. It is against the law, I realize, but hell, they been doin' it for years.

—*A California farmer*

Law Enforcement

Nowhere do farmers use child labor more openly than in Oregon's Willamette Valley. Each summer 30,000 to 35,000 children from 8 to 15 years old work in the strawberry, caneberry, and pole bean fields. Most are Oregon youngsters, recruited from schools by the state Rural Manpower Service. In 1970 state recruiters visited 523 schools and talked to 30,500 students.[1] Many of these youngsters joined the berry and bean picking crews and were bused daily from the cities into the fields. The crews—euphemistically called "platoons"—are frequently bossed by teachers who spend their summers as "platoon leaders."

In addition to these crews of city children, there are thousands of youngsters at work in the fields with their parents. These are the sons and daughters of migrant farm workers from California, Texas, and Mexico. Over the years an estimated 10,000 of these professional, seasonal farm workers have tried to settle in the Willamette Valley. They and their children are skilled farm workers.

94

Oregon farmers say they need the labor of children, that without such workers the crops could not be harvested. This "need" can be traced back to the World War II call to the colors that drained the Willamette Valley's labor supply. Those farm workers not inducted into the military found high-paying jobs in the shipyards and factories.

Historically schools in America have been attuned to the farmers' need for harvest workers. Schools traditionally end their year as the summer harvest starts. They start again in the fall after the harvests are over. During World War II growers in places like the Willamette turned to child labor. They found children could gather in the berries and beans, if you hired enough of them and didn't mind some horseplay.

As the years went by this "need" for child labor took on a character of its own. Child labor became a tradition that was summed up in a 1971 editorial in the Salem *Capital Journal*:

"Besides having the comradeship of other youth in the platoon, young pickers learn the value of the dollar and the joy of recreation earned; they gain a self-respect deep in the inner person because of having contributed to the world's needs; they help save the strawberries and beans for canning; and they have earned their own spending, clothing, and school money . . . long live the early morning sack lunches, clusters of kids waiting for platoon buses, and the honest, harmless sweat."

The editorial was a response to the American Friends Service Committee report, *Child Labor in Agriculture—Summer 1970.* AFSC investigators had gone into Oregon, Washington, California, Ohio, and Maine. In each of these states some farmers used the labor of children under circumstances that forced the investigators to conclude: "The child labor scene in 1970 is reminiscent of the sweatshop scene in 1938 . . . It should be intolerable for a sizeable segment of a major industry to depend upon child labor for its survival. In America in 1970 it is not only tolerated, it is encouraged . . . ."

The Salem *Oregon Statesman* added its editorial voice to conservative protest: "Ever so often well-meaning people from some other section of the country 'discover' that thousands of children are working in the farm fields in the Willamette Valley. Starting with the premise that all child labor is evil, they launch a campaign not just to correct the misuse of children in farm work but to beat the entire system to death with rules and regulations . . . the Willamette Valley has had trouble in the past fending off legislation in Congress designed to strangle the system which not only works to the benefit of Mid-Valley children in general, but to the farmers who would not be able to harvest their crops without youngsters."

Oregon's system is just about as unfettered as any in the nation. The child labor laws of the state generally do not apply to agriculture, with one exception. There are certain farm jobs —such as tractor driving—that are specifically designated "hazardous" and no child under the age of 16 can be employed at such work. There is an exception to the exception, however, that allows 14- and 15-year-olds to drive tractors if they have had special farm mechanics safety training.

Oregon farm apologists claim the children love to work and frolic in the berry patches. The AFSC reported, "In every instance, the children did not like the work." Picking blackberries is not a back-breaking task, nor is it a dangerous job. Any child with a small, plastic bucket can do the work. The worst that can be said is that the vines are stickery, the berries stain your fingers, the work is dull, the weather hot and sticky or damp and rainy.

Strawberries are another matter; the plants grow close to the ground, workers must kneel, crawl, bend, stoop, or sit and scrunch along, pushing a miniature wheelbarrow-like contraption that holds the "flat." One flat holds 12 quart-sized baskets and when these baskets are filled and carried to the checker, the flat is worth 80 cents to $1. This is knee-scraping, back-breaking labor. Pole beans are not much better and bush beans are worse because the full hampers weigh 30 to 35 pounds.

City children may be earning money in the farmers' fields; they may be learning the lessons of labor while helping the farmer "save" his crop at a price he can afford. But in the process these children are in direct competition with the seasonal farm workers, with those men, women, and children who must work in the fields to earn their living.

These city children are the Oregon farmers' supply of cheap, wage-depressing labor. They are recruited from Portland and Salem, from Eugene and Albany, from the full length of the Willamette Valley.

The valley is watered by the deep, slow-moving, winding Willamette River that rises in the center of the state and flows north through the gentle rolling prairies to the Columbia River. This is rich farmland. At the peak of harvest there are 60,000 seasonal farm workers employed in the rows, the vines, and the trees. The AFSC estimated children make up 75 percent of this labor force.

The 1970 Oregon Rural Manpower Service Report noted the supply of seasonal labor in the Willamette Valley was plentiful, and commented: "Two major factors contributed to this situation: (1) a strong school recruitment program for seasonal strawberry and bean harvest workers; (2) an unusually high unemployment rate which caused family units to seek and accept agricultural employment in order to maintain family income."

The response by large numbers of unemployed family workers and by large numbers of schoolchildren came crashing together into what should have been a predictable conclusion. In the Oregon City area, not far from where the Willamette River empties into the Columbia, farmers had too many workers. The RMS report said, "Some growers who had arranged for harvest platoons cancelled those arrangements disappointing several hundred schoolchildren who had been expecting work.

Since the entire north Willamette Valley was being affected by these same factors, there were no areas to which the surplus pickers could be referred.''

What happened to the migrants who came in to harvest the strawberries and beans and the local seasonal farm workers, families that were settling out of the migrant stream?

A father who was buying a rural home—a dilapidated but pleasant old farmhouse—explained: ''It was really bad this year, worse than last. Wherever we go, there are too many workers. It used to be we could start as the sun came up and we could work until dark. We are six in the family and we could make maybe $100 a day, but now there are so many people in a field they pick it clean by early in the afternoon. By then it is too late to go to another job, so you just come home.''

Machines are beginning to take over the bean crop. Farmers are converting from the hand-harvested pole beans to the bush beans that can be picked by mechanical harvesters. For the aggressive local farm worker, machines can offer steadier work and a better overall income. Traditionally these local farm workers, most of them the heads of large families, drive tractors and irrigate and act as foreman during the harvest.

But this is a tradition that is being broken. According to the 1970 RMS Report: ''It is getting increasingly difficult to find farm workers with the skill and the experience required to run the modern farm equipment who are willing to work *for the wages that the farmer is able to pay*.'' (Emphasis added.)

To help the farmer keep pay scales down, the federally funded farm advisors' office and the RMS are establishing a training session for underage farm-equipment operators. The report explained, ''The students are interested youngsters from local schools who need state permits to operate farm machinery during the summer.''

To help cut labor costs, the government is willing to train youngsters under the age of 16 to do the most dangerous work on the farm.

The Fair Labor Standards Act prohibits those under 16 from driving tractors. Oregon has a similar law. Both federal and Oregon legislators have made an exception allowing 14- and 15-year-olds to do this work after taking farm machinery safety training.

Such exceptions come at the insistence of the agri-business community and farm bloc politicians. Even then, few people in rural America seem to pay much attention to the law or the exceptions. Violations are common. When an infraction of the law is brought to public attention—usually by the injury or death of a small child—law enforcement results in little more than a token fine.

That is what happened in the case of Michael Van Hays, the 14-year-old son of a migrant farm worker, who was bounced from a tractor being driven by a 13-year-old friend. The boys were working on a Willamette Valley bean ranch alternately setting out irrigation pipe and driving the tractor. When the tractor hit a bump, Michael was thrown off. One of the large tractor tires crushed his chest. He died in a Salem hospital three hours later.

The boy was killed in August of 1970, the same summer the AFSC was investigating child labor. Both of the Salem newspapers, the *Journal* and the *Statesman*, carried short news accounts of the boy's accidental death. Seven months later the papers attacked the AFSC for its critical child labor report. The AFSC contended the use of children on farms was exploitative. The papers disagreed; the farm was a healthy, happy place for children to learn the value of labor.

Oscar Hays, Michael's father, said, "I wouldn't have let my boy go on that tractor had I knowed. My little boy went out to pick beans. They took him out of the bean field and put him on irrigation pipe."

I asked Hays if he was saying he did not know his boy was alternately riding and driving the tractor.

He was emphatic: "No sir. He went to pick beans. I've

farmed, I've worked for wages, but I never been stupid enough to put a young kid on a tractor. Any man that'd do that ought to be hung, Indian style [upside down]. Goddamn him.''

The bitterness welled up in the father's eyes, spilling tears down his cheeks. Oscar Hays and his wife are old before their time. They are white, migrant farm workers. Hays said, ''I come to California in '38, right there to the San Joaquin Valley. Lived in Lemoore and Stratford.''

The Hayses raised 13 children. Michael was the youngest. They were proud of the fact that all either had finished or would finish high school. ''We came here [Willamette Valley] to make the harvest in the berries and the beans and then we go back to California. We was just fixin' to go back when he [Michael] got killed.''

How did the accident happen?

''The kid that was drivin' the tractor, him and my little boy run around together all the time. They was real good friends. He was big for 13, bigger than my boy. I don't think he ever drove a tractor before. There was no pull bar on that tractor for them to stand on, and there was only one seat for the driver.''

According to the father, one boy would stand on the tractor's rear axle and hang on to a fender while the other boy drove. ''As the kid was driving—now how fast he was going, I don't know—he claimed he hit a chug hole, throwed my boy off in front of the tractor, thrown him off and run over him with the right hind wheel . . . .''

The Oregon Labor Bureau Wage and Hour Division administrator, A. W. Gardner, said his office and the Marion County sheriff's office investigated the case and turned the evidence over to District Attorney Gary Gortmaker. Misdemeanor labor code charges were filed; the farmer pleaded innocent and posted a $50 bond. The district attorney allowed the farmer to forfeit the bond without standing trial.

The disposition made Gardner angry: ''If a man can get off in this state or this county for $50 for a life, why then there isn't much use of me trying to go out and enforce the law.''

A year after the case had been settled Gortmaker was unavailable for comment, but Assistant District Attorney John Jensen, who handled the case, said: ''Well, the issue was not the kid's life, but that the farmer neglected to have the kids trained correctly, neglected to check their records to see if they had a permit to operate hazardous equipment. It wasn't negligent homicide. We prosecuted the farmer solely because he permitted workers to work for him that didn't have the proper experience and training.''

I pointed out that it was impossible for a 13-year-old to qualify, even with training, for such a job. Jensen agreed, ''fourteen is the cutoff. We charged him with permitting a 13-year-old to operate the tractor, right. We issued the complaint, he [the farmer] came to court, entered a not guilty plea, posted bail, and subsequently bail was forfeited.''

Jensen read me statements taken from the 13-year-old tractor driver and the ranch foreman who was supervising the boys. In substance, the statements agree with the father's account.

The boys were taken from the bean fields and put to work setting irrigation pipe.The tractor was used as transportation and apparently sometimes also to pull a trailer loaded with the aluminum pipe. According to the reports, the foreman knew the 13-year-old drove the tractor, on occasion, but the farmer had no knowledge of the fact. The foreman told investigators he was out of the field at the time of the accident, that the boys were apparently driving to a distant part of the field to fix a broken sprinkler when the tractor hit a furrow at right angles. The jolt knocked Michael's grip loose and he fell.

These words, the state labor official's anger, the assistant district attorney's explanation, were like echoes. I had heard almost the same words from the same type of officials, but in another county and in another state. A crop duster pilot had accidentally hit a 16-year-old boy as he flew low through a field. It was night, and the boy was flagging for the pilot, marking the rows for the flier to spray with pesticides.

California law prohibits the employment of 16-year-olds at night in such dangerous jobs. State labor law investigator Seward Young issued a citation, and sent the papers to the Fresno County district attorney's office. Assistant District Attorney J. H. Vallis wrote a note to Young across the bottom of the citation: "Since this is the first known offense, a warning letter should be sent to [the pilot]. If there are any future offenses, then we will prosecute."

Young, who has been in labor law enforcement too long to be surprised or get too angry, but long enough to speak his mind, said: "These cases make me feel frustrated. But even when you go to court, even when you get a conviction, like in the ice-crusher case [a teen-ager working illegally was pulled into the crusher and killed] you get a $30 fine or in the case of those 37 kids I found working in the garlic field, the contractor pled guilty and paid a $65 fine. It's almost like these guys are paying for a license to do these things."

Assistant District Attorney Vallis explained why he wrote to Young: "The labor commissioner normally first gives out a warning. If the kid had not been killed, what would have been the outcome? He [the pilot] would have simply been called in and told not to hire him. But, because of the fact the child was harmed—a fact I very much regret—they [labor law enforcement officials] want a criminal prosecution. Very seldom are these [labor law violations] brought criminally. Generally [employers] are not aware of the child labor laws, so one call by the labor commissioner sets the thing straight."

Both in Oregon and California the assistant district attorneys felt the deaths, while tragic, were coincidental to the charges, that the deaths drew attention to the violations and had this not been the case the violations would probably have gone undetected.

When cases like these occur they are reported in a few paragraphs in the local paper and forgotten. They are viewed by the general public and most government officials as simple unavoidable accidents. Most people feel the exploitation of child labor is from another time, another era. Vallis put this point of view into words: "Well, in this type of situation, it is not the same as where you have a factory where the kid is on a machine . . . we do know at the time most [of the child labor laws] came out, children worked in various hazardous occupations 12 hours a day, with very little sleep, little food, where they were subjected to real dangers every minute of their existence. Labor conditions in those times were absolutely horrendous. This, of course, was a long time ago. Thank God we don't have those conditions now . . . ."

Americans simply do not consider the farm a dangerous place to work, nor child labor a harmful experience if that work is performed on the farm. In rural communities the judges, school officials, employers, and even some of the farm workers, argue that such work keeps the kids off the street and teaches them the lessons of labor.

Farmers who are decent men, who oppose exploitation of children, who work hard themselves and face grave economic crisis, still argue the myths of child labor. As a result the legal and illegal use of child labor in agriculture has become part of a complex, historical pattern which also ignores minimum wage laws and social security regulations.

In theory the combination of state and federal laws establishes a strict protective framework around children. But it doesn't always work out that way. California has the most stringent and the most complex child labor laws in the nation.

Any child who is going to work for any employer other than his own parents must be 12 years old, must have a work permit from local school officials, cannot work while school is in session, and cannot work at a long list of hazardous jobs.

During the school year children who are 14 or older and who have completed the eighth grade can get special permission to work if the family is in desperate need. There are other exceptions, including one that allows 14- and 15-year-olds to drive tractors if they have had special training. But the regulations and the exceptions have been written to make it difficult for a child to escape an education.

Yet they do. Leo Lopez, chief of the California migrant education programs, estimated there are 40,000 school-age youngsters who are invisible to government record-keeping agencies. These youngsters are presumed to be working, or babysitting so their parents can work, or they don't have shoes or clothes to wear to school.

In just one of California's 200 crops (raisin grapes) labor law investigator Seward Young estimated 30 percent of the 35,000 harvest workers were children under 12. This would mean 10,000 or more children working illegally in September before school starts. If the crop is late, some rural school officials will delay the opening a week or more so the children, working legally or illegally, may continue the harvest.

After school has started, the federal wage and hour officials have jurisdiction under the Fair Labor Standards Act. In five days in the fall of 1971 two federal investigators found 82 children working in tomatoes, figs, and raisin grapes on 25 San Joaquin Valley farms.

In a week's tour from the San Joaquin Valley northward 250 miles, up through the coastal valleys above San Francisco, I saw 125 children working illegally in the chili peppers, grapes, apples, and prunes. Most were with their parents, but one crew was made up almost entirely of children from 6 to 15 years old.

These 20 children were working on the same large apple ranch as their parents, but they were working as a separate crew, under the supervision of one or two adults. I had gone north just to find them, because I had heard they had gone on strike. They had been earning 7 cents a bucket and had asked for a penny more.

When the youngsters made their demand, I was told the crew boss took their pay cards—for each bucket they received a hole punched in a pay card—and told them to return to the labor camp. That night the word was spread throughout the camp that if the kids were not back at work in the morning the families would be asked to move out. The strike was broken, the children went back to work at the 7-cent rate.

We drove onto the ranch just after noon, and found that the crew of children had finished their lunches and were climbing back on the tractor-drawn flatbed trailers used to haul apple bins out of the orchards. (It is against California law to allow anyone under 16 to be in, on, or around moving machinery.) We followed the trailers into the orchard, up over a gentle hill, and down to where the youngsters had left off. As soon as the tractors stopped, the children went to work. They carry their buckets from tree to tree, scurrying about like squirrels after nuts. They work with both hands, picking apples off the ground and throwing them into the buckets. When a bucket is full it is emptied into a large bin and the crew leader punches their ticket.

We watched awhile, took a few pictures, then left. I was being guided by a farm worker who knew the area and the people. That evening we returned to the ranch to talk to the families. It turned out that the leader of the abortive strike was a pretty Mexican teen-ager, the daughter of migrant parents who each spring drive 1,800 miles from their home in Zacatecas, Mexico, to California's apple country near Sonoma.

The first work is thinning fruit on the trees, so that what is left can mature to marketable size and quality. After the thinning this family drives north, another 300 or 400 miles, into the Willamette Valley to work in the strawberries. In midsummer they return to the California summer apples, then prunes, and finally the late fall apple harvest. They try to return to Zacatecas by Christmas.

The father works on the ladders in the trees and can earn $20 to $25 a day. His wife and five children pick the fruit off the ground at seven cents a bucket. Together they can gather around 270 buckets a day—that is $18.90 for six ground workers. The youngest is 8 years old.

I asked the daughter about the strike. She said it hadn't been a strike, they hadn't walked out or set up picket lines. They had simply asked the crew leader for more money. She was polite, but defiant—not quite sure she should be talking to a stranger, but not willing to show she was afraid of any Anglo's questions.

Earlier in the year the family had been working in the Oregon strawberries for 85 cents a flat, but it was not enough. So the crew of 180 men, women, and children stopped work and asked for $1 a flat. The fruit was ripe and the farmer anxious. He agreed.

"The strike we made in Oregon was in my mind. In the apples we have been getting 7 cents for at least 10 years. So I started telling the others we should get more. There were some Anglo kids working near us, but they didn't want to strike. They wouldn't agree, so it was only us Mexicans who made the strike."

Why had the effort failed?

"The Anglos wouldn't come with us."

As she talked her father chuckled and shook his head. He was obviously pleased with the girl, and amused. The strike in Oregon had worked because the farmer was not in a position to argue. The strike in the apples had carried no such threat. He himself had had to take a cut in the piece rate this past season because the farmers in the area had set the rate lower.

It is common for crews to stop work and ask for higher pay if their numbers are great enough and the crop is ripe enough and there is little chance the farmer can bring in other workers quickly. Otherwise, there is no use trying by threat.

The word "strike" and the appearance of any outside organizational effort make California farmers very nervous. Since 1965, when Filipino and Chicano table-grape workers went out on strike in Delano, the farmers have become more sensitive to workers' requests and demands. This sensitivity can erupt in anger and dismissals, or it can be turned into a lever by nonunion farm workers seeking higher pay.

I asked the defiant, pretty little Mexican teen-ager what she thought of Cesar Chavez, leader of the United Farm Workers Union.

Without hesitation she answered, "He's one of our finest."

Her jaw thrust out, her feet were planted a bit apart, almost as if she expected a fight. She was a Chicana—a proud Mexicana—and nobody was going to make her back down. She believed in the UFWU, the strikes, and the boycotts.

Her attitude was exceptional. The display of such feeling to an outsider was something I had not seen among the migrants who come up out of Florida and Texas to work the eastern and midwestern crops. But such aggressive behavior is becoming more evident in California, where Chavez and the UFWU are part of the agricultural scene.

The Union is having an effect on the use of child labor in this state. Farmers in the San Joaquin Valley, who bitterly oppose Chavez and the union, know that Chicano farm-working families depend upon the work of their children to supplement family income. Some of these farmers are telling the workers that because of the union activities, they can no longer allow children in the fields and orchards. And where the UFWU has contracts, employment is restricted to union members. To join the Union a worker must be at least 16 years old.

The UFWU position is obvious: Farm wages must be high enough so a man can earn enough to support his family. But union officials do not make an issue of child labor and many of the union members take their entire families into crops that are not yet organized.

As in most other farm states, an exact count of California farm workers is impossible. The state Rural Manpower Service estimates the peak at 375,000. But its estimates are based on the amount of labor a crop theoretically needs. If it takes 10 man-weeks of labor to produce a specific acreage of peaches, then the RMS marks down 10 men working one week in that crop. It then estimates 16 percent or so of these are migrants. The state migrant health service reports there are 485,000 farm workers in the state at the peak of the harvest.

Whatever the number, these workers break up into several distinct farm labor forces. There are the Anglo cherry pickers, the self-styled "rubber tire tramps" who winter in the olives and citrus of the central San Joaquin Valley and then in May move north into the cherry harvests. They follow the cherries and the apples into Oregon and Washington. Some branch off to the northeast before returning to the late fall olive harvest.

There are the Chicano tree-fruit workers who move up and down the San Joaquin and Sacramento Valleys; the vegetable workers who never go into the trees if they can help it; the melon workers who live in Mexico and work north through the state. Some crops, like lettuce, use few families.

There are people who work only in the vines, who harvest grapes, who prune and tie the vines, and complete the other cultural practices needed to bring the fruit in fresh, or for wine or raisins.

There are the settled-out families. They live in the cities, the men work as janitors or street sweepers, the women and children day haul out to the fields. Each summer, during the peak of harvest, the father takes his vacation and the family travels into the grapes or the peaches.

The State Migrant Health Office estimates there are 160,000 migrants within the California farm labor force. These are the families and single workers that move from one crop to another, from one part of the state to another, and from one school district to another in order to find work.

Because family farm labor housing is so bad—a 1963 report by a special governor's committee indicated 80 percent of the farm worker families lived in grossly substandard housing, that one-third of the houses had no flush toilet, nearly a third had no bath, and 25 percent had no running water at all—the state, using $7,000,000 in federal funds, built 26 seasonal farm labor camps. The camps, ranging from 50 to 150 units each, are called "flash peak housing"; they are boxlike cabins that have two partitioned "bedrooms," a tiny living room–kitchen, and a bathroom that contains a toilet bowl and shower. These 20-by-25 foot cabins have no form of cooling and become unbearable ovens in the 103-degree San Joaquin Valley summertime temperatures.

There are 2,780 families (14,500 men, women, and children) living in these federally funded, state-owned, county-operated camps each season. Most come in the early spring, as the camps open, and stay until late fall, when the camps close. During the season the camp managers turn away from 3,000 to 4,000 families. The camps are popular, primarily because of the low rents. The camps also provide preschool child-care centers, central laundries, and health-care clinics.

Twenty-five percent of the families housed in the camps come here directly from Mexico each season, another 35 percent are Mexicans or Mexican-Americans from Texas' Rio Grande Valley. California migrants make up 34 percent of the camp population, and most of these families are either Mexican aliens here on visas or Mexican-Americans from other parts of the state.

The average migrant family in these camps earns $3,019 a year. This includes the earnings of the children. Because the camp day care facilities are limited to preschool-age children, most of the children who are over 6 years old go to the fields with their parents. Some attend migrant summer schools in nearby school districts.

The Mexican families in these camps represent only a small portion of the total foreign labor pool within California farming. Thousands of families come in each year; most must find housing in private labor camps, or in rentals in the barrios (ghettos) that surround most cities in the farming areas.

Up and down the San Joaquin and Sacramento Valleys there are tiny communities, farm worker shantytowns where former migrants are trying to settle. Out-of-state migrants come into these communities seeking a friend or a cousin or a brother who already lives there. If there is work, if they "make it pretty good" for a season, they will stay over and begin to think about settling.

For years farm workers in these shanty communities would buy a shack and then make additions as they could afford to. Nothing else was available. During the 1960's an American Friends Service Committee self-help housing project developed into Self Help Enterprises, a federally assisted program that has allowed 1,000 farm worker families to build their own $15,000 homes.

Most migrants have not been so fortunate. Like José Sanchez, they arrived in California with only what they could carry. Sanchez, a young father of five, said: "We were in Casa Grande, Arizona, and it was a question of whether we went broke in Texas or in California. We had never been to California before.

"We had heard from a friend in Lodi you could make it pretty good. I was just married then about two years, we had just one child. There was also my father and mother, and my four brothers. We had about $120 between us. I was driving an old '54 Ford with one light pointing up and the other light pointing down. It was cockeyed, you know? My father had a pickup and he was pulling an old trailer with all the chivas [family belongings].''

The Sanchez family followed the same route as the Joad family in *The Grapes of Wrath*, two decades before; they drove up over the Tehachapi Mountains and down into the San Joaquin Valley.

In Bakersfield, they turned north on Highway 99. "My father was following me, because I had to drive so slowly. My front wheels were not too straight and when I would go fast, the car would shake pretty bad. Anyway, we were by Tipton, going slow when I see a wheel—just a wheel and a tire on it—go by me fast. It was going right down the white line. Cars were going crazy trying to get out of the way.

"It scared me, you know? I looked in the mirror and I see my father's car with the trailer skidding without a wheel. I looked up and that damn wheel was still going. I think it would have gone to Lodi by itself if it hadn't turned and gone off and hit the railroad tracks.

"It went up the bank and bounced way up in the air. It took us a while to find it. We got the wheel back, but it was broken so we had to go to a junkyard. We were lucky, we found another wheel and other parts we needed and it only cost $2.''

The family arrived in Lodi in midwinter, without funds. They found their friends, who in turn found them a place to stay . . . an old barn. "They gave us enough food and we managed to get along until we found some work thinning the onions. I remember I made $12 the first day.''

The family moved again that spring, south to the Woodville Farm Labor Center, a migrant camp operated by the Tulare County Housing Authority. The farm labor center was built in 1939 by the USDA's Farm Security Administration to meet a critical depression-era migrant housing shortage. Most of the camp was devoted to 185 one-room tin shelters. It cost only

$100 to build one of these 16-by-20-foot, single-wall, metal shelters. The windows were nothing more than screened openings that could be "closed" by shutters made of the same material as the walls. There was no glass.

Each shelter contained one gas outlet and several electrical outlets. Nothing else. Water was outside and down the street; the faucets were located next to the garbage can racks. Great, barnlike structures served as central toilet and shower rooms; there were also central laundry areas and a camp auditorium or meeting hall.

Dozens of these old camps were still being operated in Florida, Texas, Washington, and California during the 1960's. They all were in horrible shape, the plumbing was outdated and so badly worn it was all but inoperable; in one California county, health inspectors found it was possible for the urinals to back up into the camp's drinking-water supply. These camps were condemned for this and a dozen other health conditions considered too extensive to repair. Such condemnations eventually doomed most of these camps—30 years after they had been built as temporary shelters.

Sanchez recalled, "We would work in Tulare County grapes, and the citrus, and during the winter we would prune the vines. In the spring we would hear 'you can make it pretty good' in Yuba City in the peaches and plums and we'd pack up and go [300 miles] north. But we would pay two months' rent [$50] first, so we would have a place when we got back, because one time there was no cabin when we came into camp. We had to wait 15 days living in the grass beside the road. One of the ladies in a cabin near us let us use her stove, but we had to wait that long to get a cabin."

Each summer they returned to the same farm north of Sacramento. "We found the best rancher in Sutter County. He would pay us $1 or $1.50 more than the others, and he didn't want you to fill his bin so full. We all would work, even the kids. We give them buckets and they help fill the bins.

"We would get up at four o'clock, the women would cook something, but we wouldn't eat then. We would go into the field at five or five-thirty and work until ten, then eat. We would have some little things for the kids to eat and some soda for them to drink, but we wouldn't eat again until we got back about four in the afternoon."

Why drive so far, when the same kind of work was available closer?

A pattern, a habit had been formed. They went where they knew they could get work and a premium offered by the grower. Sanchez said, "Our track was narrow. We had Highway 99, the camp in Woodville, and the jobs in Yuba City. Most of the talk when we went up was about the job, about how much we could make for the season."

Today Sanchez has a regular job, with a steady income. His wife and children no longer must go into the fields, though in the summertime they do, to earn money for their school clothes. The family has been off the migrant pathways now for nearly three years. There is hope they will buy a home of their own. I asked Sanchez to remember back to the migrant days. Were there any good times?

"Why sure. The good times are when you don't have any extraordinary problems. If you are not sick, real sick, and you are working a little bit and you can go to a movie once in a while, those are the good times.

"If I could make ends meet, then it was all right with me. Things were good. I think I would not change agriculture work for any other, it can be just as good as an assembly line in Detroit, maybe better."

To many who must still scratch and struggle for a living traveling with the crops, men like Sanchez have "made it." Most have not. A California migrant health report in 1970 observed: "One-third of all the farm workers available for full-time work nevertheless spend more than half the year unemployed." Having this kind of labor surplus is to the farmers' advantage.

Such figures explain why thousands of hard-working seasonal farm laborers must seek welfare during the winter months when there is no work. There is no other way. Farmers have never allowed farm labor unemployment insurance programs to be enacted. The result is increased welfare loads.

Although California's welfare system has been one of the most liberal in the nation, getting relief if you are a migrant farm worker or a permanent resident worker can be a trying experience. In Madera County a California Rural Legal Assistance lawyer asked farmers who were receiving from $5,000 to $133,000 in federal crop subsidies what they thought about various forms of welfare for the poor. Over half (57 percent) were opposed to welfare programs as they existed, 81 percent opposed the idea of a guaranteed annual income of $4,500 for a family of seven.

The wife of a grower receiving $16,000 in federal crop subsidies said, "I can't understand having things handed to you."

A grower who was receiving $8,000 said, "Idleness causes many evils."

The conservative atmosphere in the state is obviously not confined to the rural hinterlands. On the subject of child labor, the pressures start right from the top, with Governor Ronald Reagan.

In 1968 an internal memo went out to all labor law enforcement area supervisors: "The [Reagan] administration is currently interested in enabling youth to seek and obtain employment without restrictive barriers . . . ." The memo asked for suggestions on how this might be accomplished.

One area supervisor said, "We got the message loud and clear. 'Slack off.' "

At the same time the governor's budget-cutting eliminated almost half the labor law enforcement investigative staff. Only twelve slots were left, and four of the men in these positions resigned in disgust. Morale was at its lowest.

In the spring of 1972, a legislative committee poking around the State Department of Industrial Relations—the parent of the labor law enforcement division—was told DIR Director William C. Hern had been cited for labor code violations 19 times prior to being appointed by Reagan. When the news broke, the Los Angeles *Times* editorially called for Hern's ouster, noting that a deputy commissioner of Hern's department had testified in a legislative committee hearing that Hern had followed "a calculated program . . . to decimate, demoralize, and immobilize" the state's labor law enforcement program.

But the pressures on investigators came not only from the top state administrators, they also came from within the agribusiness community as well. Investigator Seward Young said, "My biggest problem is with the judges."

In August of 1971 Young cited two labor contractors in the Fresno area for hiring 120 children under 12 years old to harvest chili peppers. The children were working with their parents. One of the contractors pleaded guilty and was fined $50 on each of the two counts. The other contractor, Raul Torrez, pleaded innocent. Before he went to trial, Young and I inspected his fields again. There were 50 families in the field. By Young's estimate there were from 60 to 80 children under 12 working. The contractor took us to the grader, a portable, shedlike affair where workers brought the chili peppers to be weighed, sorted, and loaded onto a truck.

"Look," Torrez pointed to hand-lettered cardboard signs warning the parents in both Spanish and English that they could not bring their young children into the fields to work. "It's impossible to keep those kids out of there, I've told 'em, I've put signs up. What more can I do?"

Torrez went to his pickup, motioning us to follow. He pulled out a legal pad of yellow-ruled paper. On it someone had printed: "The undersigned names request section 1290 of the labor code be waived." Below that were lists of signatures. Torrez explained, ''There are 75 names on there, the parents'; they don't want the law. [Section 1290 sets the 12-year-old age limit.] They want their kids to be able to work.''

Chili pepper plants grow low to the ground. The peppers as they mature are picked by hand. Growers pay from 2 to 5 cents a pound, depending upon the variety and the size of the crop.

Torrez was paying $1 a 45-pound sack. There were so many workers in this particular field their sacks were stacked up at the grader and the sorters there could not keep up. Torrez shut the field down shortly after noon, so they could catch up.

Young and I watched the last hour of work. The families work together, the father setting each member of his family in a row. The smallest children pick into their mother's sack. When the sacks are full, they are either carried to the edge of the row or left standing in the field to be carried out at the end of the day.

When Torrez signaled the crew he was calling a halt to the picking, the workers finished the sacks they were working on and began carrying them out of the fields.

The smallest children gathered up picking baskets, lunch sacks, and Thermos bottles while the older children and their parents bent to the heavy work. One frail-looking boy in glasses reached down and put both arms around one of the 45-pound sacks, he squeezed hard and reared back. He waddled a few steps and the sack slipped. He stumbled, half falling. Again he wrapped his arms around the sack and struggled down the row.

Farther down the field, a tough little 9-year-old knelt by a sack, tipped it over on his right shoulder, and straightened up; with his right hand on his hip and his elbow akimbo, he balanced the load exactly like his father, who had just walked out ahead of him. When this boy walked past, I reached over, hefted the sack off his shoulder, and set it down. Then I lifted him. He and the sack were about the same weight. I helped him carry it to the car where his father was stacking the day's work sacks on the rear of the car so they could be driven the half-mile to the grader.

As the families turned in their sacks and received their money, Young and I noticed many were disgruntled. Some of the young teen-agers were angry. We stopped several and asked what had happened. The knew the pay was low—the chili is not known as a good crop—but they hadn't realized how poorly they all had done. The workers we watched had averaged 40 to 80 cents an hour.

We looked at three other chili fields that day, and the story was about the same in each. In addition to child labor law violations, we saw entire families being paid off on a single social security card account number. Obviously the employers were not meeting the state minimum wage of $1.65 for women and minors.

Chili farmer Joe Leonetti, of Fresno, who hires a contractor to recruit and supervise the crews, but who pays the workers himself, was asked if he took down a social security number for each worker.

"No. No, you just take it from the father, or whoever does the weighing-in. It is usually the father."

Asked about minimum wages, Leonetti said, "I understand it is $1.65 an hour, but how you goin' to figure that out? I think it is silly. I picked grapes for a cent and a half a tray when I was a kid."

The State Division of Industrial Welfare is charged with the responsibility of checking minimum wage violations and with enforcing the payroll record-keeping requirements; social security is a federal responsibility, handled by the Internal Revenue Service; child labor laws are enforced by state labor law enforcement investigators like Young.

Young also must police labor contractor regulations and the

field sanitation provisions (chemical toilets, fresh drinking water, hand washing facilities), as well as all labor laws operable in the cities.

When I checked with the DIW and other agencies they all had reasons why they did not go into the field to seek out violations. In the end I concluded that the men from Young's office were the only ones who aggressively police the laws in their jurisdiction.

When you consider there are only 12 investigators within the labor law enforcement division to cover the entire state, the task seems awesome. Young's territory covers 9 counties, an area about the size of New York State.

I asked if there was anyone he could call on to help him. Were there any other agencies sympathetic enough to the work to give him a hand when he needed it?

He was silent for ten seconds, then asked me to repeat the question.

I asked again if there was anyone who would help him, who could for example pinpoint child labor violations and report them.

He was silent for another six seconds, then said, "No. There's no one."

Men like Seward Young are alone in an unpopular field of law. Not even the conservative justice court judges who routinely lecture on law and order to those who pass under their gavel will help out.

When labor contractor Raul Torrez went into Fresno Municipal Court for his trial on charges of hiring children under 12, the district attorney's office was unprepared. The assistant district attorney said the court had failed to notify him of the trial date.

Young is normally served notice, too, but in this instance he was not. He showed up anyway. Before a formal hearing was started on the charges, Judge Mikio Uchiyama and Torrez discussed the case. Torrez explained the parents bring the children to the field despite the signs and verbal warnings.

The court reporter, though unprepared because the hearing had not started, began taking sketchy notes because obviously something was about to happen. It did. The judge agreed with Torrez. He dismissed the charges.

I talked to the judge later, asking why he had let Torrez go.

Judge Uchiyama explained, "The work was being done by the parents on the piece rate. It is up to the parents to determine whether or not the children work. The contractor had made the agreement with the parents and was paying the parents, not the children."

The law is specific. It is the employer's responsibility to determine if a child in the field has a work permit issued by the local school district. Section 11270 of the state education codes allows the employer to post notices against child labor to protect himself, but specifically the law requires him to make the work permit check on children he sees working.

And the labor code, section 1304, says, "Failure to produce permits to work or to employ is prima facie evidence of illegal employment of minors." The law does not leave it up to the parents' discretion or the labor contractor's discretion.

Other judges in the San Joaquin Valley feel as Judge Uchiyama does. Stockton Municipal Judge Chris Pappas only placed a labor contractor on probation on charges he was working three children, aged 8, 11, and 15, in the tomato harvest while school was in session.

The judge explained the parents, "itinerant fruit workers of Indian extraction" were from Parker, Arizona, and were here trying to make a living. The contractor had hired the parents, not the children. The parents obviously didn't have the funds to hire a babysitter, so they took the kids to the field. Judge

Pappas asked: "After all, how many tomatoes can an eight-year-old pick?"

The issue before his court was the employment of minors while school was in session, but the judge didn't see it that way. Instead, he felt the labor law enforcement officers were picking on a labor contractor "to build their record in Sacramento."

Judge Paul E. Howard of the Firebaugh Justice Court in the San Joaquin Valley: "My opinion, and most of my decisions, are based on the fact that I believe they should allow—not only allow, but foster—the use of minors and juveniles in farm work."

Farmer Leonetti put it this way: "They [state labor law enforcement agents] make a big deal out of nothing. These kids are happy out there working."

6

I wish they'd go to school [but] our schools don't
want to bother with them . . . [school officials]
are supposed to come out if the kids aren't in school
and see what happened to them, but they don't.
—*An Ohio farmer*

Lección, Escritura, y Aritmética

"La sistema de la escuela de América trabaja
mejor cuando los administradores y maestros de la clase de
medio hablan a los estudiantes de la misma clase con los mismos
orientaciones. La clase de abajo y los estudiantes minoridades
que no acaben en el moho no van estar educados y mas o
menos van a ser conjunto de datos que no terminan escuela."

To those who do not read Spanish, the words of David Ballesteros have no meaning. The shock of being unable to understand what he is saying is irritating. In a very small way it
is like the 5- and 6-year-old Mexican children entering school
in Texas or California or Ohio and hearing the teacher issuing
orders in the confusing sounds of the English language.

Ballesteros is an American of Mexican descent, a college
professor who is culturally and linguistically a Mexicano. The
bilingual reader can detect in Ballesteros' words a strong feeling
that the middle-class educational system has failed the Spanish-
speaking minorities. The educator is critical of the American

121

schools because to succeed students must be comfortable within the middle-class value system. As a result, Ballesteros said, "La educación lograda el alumno hispano parlante en los Estados Unidos está cuatro años atrás de anglo-norteamericano y dos años atrás de las otras minorías." (The education of the Spanish-speaking students in the United States is four years behind the North-American Anglo and two years behind other minorities.)[1]

Ballesteros' words have a special meaning in the rural areas, in the colonias and barrios where the seasonal farm workers live, and out in the labor camps where they must stay when they are traveling from crop to crop. From the migrants' home bases in Florida, in Texas, and in California, the reports show the Black and the Chicano children begin serious work in the crops when they are between 9 and 12 years old and that soon thereafter they begin to drop out of school.

These children don't fit into the carefully constructed middle-class molds created by the American schools. They live in an unstable, constantly shifting environment. Nothing they touch or feel or see has any permanency. Life is an unbroken series of crises. There is little incentive to plan ahead. That tomorrow will bring unexpected problems there can be no doubt, but first there is the rent to pay. There is not enough food in the house, the car is broken down and must be fixed so the family can go to work, two of the children need shoes, and the oldest daughter is crying because the one school dress she has is too small and too tight. The high school dean of women has scolded her and sent her home, telling her not to come back until she can dress decently, modestly.

For such children home is a series of discarded shanties, old buses, crowded barracks buildings that were declared surplus after World War II, then cut up and moved out onto a remote alkali flat or back under some trees, next to a swamp. Partitions were framed in to make "apartments" and the buildings have been "family" housing for a quarter-century.

The toilets are foul-smelling pit privies, the bathrooms communal concrete-and-wood showers that stink of urine and mold. Drinking and cooking water comes from faucets that sprout out of a muddy puddle of water in the campyard or from the cracked washtubs hanging on the bathhouse wall.

Inside these dimly lit "homes" there is never enough room for the large family. The floors sag underfoot, there are no cupboards, no bookshelves, no books or magazines or newspapers. Except for religious artifacts and pictures of Martin Luther King, of Robert and John Kennedy, the walls are unadorned. In one corner, on an old TV, there will be photos of the family, of a son killed in Vietnam, of a daughter's wedding. But private, transferable possessions are few.

There are few toys, and those are usually broken hand-me-downs that belong to no single child. The children own nothing individually, even their clothing is shared. They have little or no experience with blocks or games or crayons. But they are inventive. They create toys out of the camp litter, the cast-off scraps of migrant life.

Within the cabins and rental apartments in the rural agri-slums there are never enough knives and forks, the table is too small, and there aren't enough chairs for the family to sit down together at mealtime. Food is often a catch-as-catch-can thing; dinner is cooked and the children get a plate or a cup, fill it, and wander off to a corner to eat. If the family is working, there may be some meat in the meal, if they are not and times are really rough, dinner may only be potato-peel soup.

In the early mornings the parents go off to work, the children get themselves ready for school. For breakfast they may have a cup of coffee or a soda pop with a cream-filled cake or cocoa syrup sandwiches. Unless the school provides lunches free, the next meal is a prowl through the food boxes after school.

Very little in their lives prepares these children for school. A California text on health, written for third graders, directs the student to "think of the names of the foods you ate for breakfast, lunch, and dinner yesterday,'' and then to write them down in columns under the appropriate heading. Teachers then follow this up with oral reports. One by one the students stand and explain what they have eaten. The migrant children not only get to hear what the town kids eat—and thereby learn once again how different, how poor they are—they face the awful task of getting up and confessing the family poverty.

A Chicano teacher, a former seasonal farm worker, said, "I really remember those things, like once the first day in school—it was the fourth or fifth grade—the teacher asked each student to say his name and what he had done for vacation.

"This one had gone to Yosemite, that one had been in an airplane, another one went for a long trip. We picked grapes and peaches. That's all. So when it was my turn, I guess I said, 'We didn't do anything,' but I guess I didn't say it loud enough, because she made me say it again.

"My brother was sitting right behind me. He almost yelled, 'Next year we're going to buy a boat and we're going to go everywhere.' Everybody laughed at the way he said it. I don't know where he got the idea, I don't think he'd even been close to a boat, but he had to say something.''

The Chicano teacher went on to explain what poverty means to a student. In junior and senior high schools there are small charges for student-body cards, for club dues, for athletic insurance. There is a daily need for lunch money, field trips cost extra sometimes, there are workbook and lab-book fees. These are routine, inconsequential—unless you are poor.

José, a 17-year-old high school senior from Texas wanted very much to graduate from high school, but he doubted he could make it. He is a serious kid who plays football and is pinning his hopes for college on a football scholarship. But first he must stay in school. His problem is not grades—he gets above-average marks—but economics. He is the oldest and is expected to help out on the family finances.

José said, "I owe $6 from last year's FFA dues and for this year, but I've already paid $13 in football insurance.

"We didn't do too well up North. I found a job driving a cotton-picking machine this fall down here so I am making a little extra, but we have to pay the bills and my father is sick."

The Future Farmers of America dues are part of the vocational agriculture course; the dues are $3 a year "and if you don't pay the teacher gets real mad at you and tells you you have to clean out the hog pens. You gotta get in the pens with the hogs and you got on your good school clothes." José cannot afford a pair of coveralls and the only footwear he has is an old pair of shoes he bought last year. Even though the Anglo teacher is harsh, José stays in the vocational agriculture course because he is learning welding. "Maybe I can get a job welding weekends or after school, that way I can finish and go on to college and still help my family."

The majority of the students in José's high school are aliens or Mexican-Americans; he estimates 40 percent of them go north to work each year and return to school late in the fall. The school is a typical middle-class establishment, run by an Anglo principal and an Anglo superintendent who both wear their hair close-cropped in crew cuts and who insist the Spanish-speaking students conform to similar short-hair standards.

José said, "If they see a Chicano guy with long hair, they go after him, but if they see an American with long hair, they don't say anything."

From his conversation and from talks with the school officials it became obvious the school was no worse than most: Anglo-norteamericano middle-class values prevail. This is the system that teaches English by banning Spanish. This is the system that conveys the neat, orderly, well-financed suburban atmosphere where competition is the key to success. This is the system that is benevolently brought to the poor—or the poor are transported to it. This is the system run by $20,000- to $30,000-a-year Anglos who owe their jobs to school boards made up of doctors, lawyers, farmers, realtors.

Narcisio, a 22-year-old college freshman, said: "You learn quick to do it their way, the Anglo way. You try, you know, because you want to belong. One day you think you are going to settle down and you are going to make it and the only way to make it is the gabacho way. This was a big thing with our family because we never owned a home. It has always been one camp or another.

"Even my kid brothers who are still in school now, when they come back from school it is to a goddamn camp. But it's more than a camp. It's a life-style. You are only going to school because of the legal system. The camp is a working atmosphere, you make a buck out in the field and you eat and sleep and go out again. You go to school only because they grab you and put you in school."

Narcisio still considers himself a migrant, although he now attends college on a federally funded scholarship. As a child he traveled with his parents and his brothers and sisters over much of the eastern half of the United States. Late in the fall they would return to a small town southwest of Lake Okeechobee and work in Florida's winter vegetables. It was here he went to school.

"At home you open a book and out comes a cockroach, man that really sticks in your mind. The goddamn bugs. In junior high school and high school, I don't care how poor you are, you try, man, you try to have a good pair of blue jeans and a good shirt, neatly ironed and all, and you try to assimilate, you try to be a part of the class, but when you get back home, it's a goddamn camp."

The way Narcisio says those last three words, the way he repeats them, expresses a hatred and resentment that is hard to describe. Narcisio is considered a militant Chicano, an organizer who would have junior high school and high school students demand that school officials pay attention to their needs.

"It's a problem. Your father cannot make enough money and even if you all work Saturday and Sunday you never quite have enough. I can remember clearly in the second and third and fourth grades we never had the money to buy the workbooks that went with the hardcover textbooks. It sounds like a little thing, but the other kids had the workbooks to write and color in and to make words, but shit, we never had that.

"The only shoes I wore in the second grade were boots that we got from the welfare. That was the only welfare item we expected, was shoes for us so we could go to school, but once in a while we would need some of that surplus food when my father was out of work. But we hated that, man, because they made you feel so bad when they gave it to you."

Narcisio is one of a small percentage of migrant students who finish high school. "Man, I was a long ways behind, though. We missed a year, a whole goddamn year when we moved from Texas over here. Man, we didn't have a thing, not a thing. We slept in the truck. The women would sleep up under the canvas top and the men would sleep on the ground. If it was raining we would get underneath the truck, but it was muddy as hell. We found some work then, and we got into a camp."

Narcisio is obviously very bright, very aggressive. He is also a manipulator who is used to talking to the Anglo world. He spends much of his time working in a militant Chicano organization and he travels extensively, talking to students.

"When I went to college, it all hit me. I hadn't seen so much glass and so much concrete in all my life. I got the loan and I rented a dormitory room, a whole room, man, all to myself. It had wall-to-wall carpet, and air conditioning. It was something fantastic. I'd never seen anything like it, and I strived man, I really wanted to be a college kid.

"But then I went back home, to that camp, and I saw my brothers struggling, I saw the cockroaches and the rats. It is really sad to see somebody get all involved like I was; you go back on weekends and work in the fields, drive a tractor or pick some oranges. But you hate it. You get accustomed to comfortable beds and everything is so much cleaner.

"When I went back to the camp, I just couldn't stand it and I took it out on everybody in the family." Narcisio stopped talking. He had been traveling all day, he was tired, and the memories and emotions were rushing in on him too fast.

He looked up and asked, "Why couldn't we have had a bed that had four posts instead of tomato boxes holding it up? Why not a kitchen table with chairs around it, instead of tomato boxes with boards between them? Why did we have to go to school where they used to send the Black kids before desegregation was ordered? You should have seen those old buildings, and you know they gave us textbooks that were 20 years old?"

Education for a child of the fields is a sometime thing, dependent entirely upon the season, the weather, and the location, as well as the daily economic fate of the family. For the Black child there is the added stigma of race, of the nigger-slave stereotype. Even with an education the job opportunities are limited.

One Black Florida youth put it this way: "Guys go off and get one or two years of college and they still can't get a job, not around here [Belle Glade].

"You can go to Miami or some other big city and what've you got? Maybe a job at the airport, or a warehouse or maybe one cutting glass for $65 or $70 a week. Now that's not what you call good wages. So what the hell's the use?"

This teen-ager wears a subdued Afro hair style. He's tall and muscular and was once an outstanding athlete. "Some of these guys on the street [dropouts] have some neat rags and the kids in school they see this, so they aren't too enthused about school. Some of these kids think that being on the street is the real thing.

"They don't see how it's important to stay in school. They see the dudes goin' North an' somebody says, 'Come on with us, we'll make some money and we'll find some girls up in New Jersey' and that's it, they leave."

For the Spanish-speaking child there is the extra problem of learning another language before he or she can understand what is going on in the classroom. Alfonso Ramirez, director of a migrant education bilingual research project in the Rio Grande Valley, said, "First I want you to understand I feel the migrant and the nonmigrant have the same needs. The Mexican-American child who goes North shares the same educational needs as the one who stays.

"It is only in the first years of school that the non-English-speaking children get an opportunity to practice English in the classroom. From the fourth and fifth grades on we don't know how to teach children to speak, so for all practical purposes the child is attending class and sitting there and never has much to say.

"The whole setup in classrooms is traditional, the desks in long rows in cavernous rooms, the teacher up front. Speaking is discouraged, rather than encouraged. In most situations he [the farm worker child] is pretty much a spectator in the classroom, rather than a participant."

Ramirez works out of Edinburg, the Hidalgo County seat. The concentration of migrants is greater here than anywhere else in the nation. Three cities here—Pharr, San Juan, and Alamo—operate a unified school district that has one high school, two junior highs and thirteen elementary schools.

In the fall, when school starts, the student enrollment is 7,100. By Christmas vacation there are 10,000 students in the schools of these three small towns. Then, by the 30th week of school the numbers fall rapidly. In mid-May there are again 7,100 students in school.

The Pharr–San Juan–Alamo district operates both the federally funded migrant 6-month schools and the 10-month traditional classes. The migrant classes concentrate a full 10-months curriculum into the shorter period by extending the class day. Classes start at 8 a.m. and end at 5 p.m.

Assistant District Superintendent Agusto Guerra said the children who enter the first grade speaking only Spanish are usually held over an extra year so they can "catch up" after they learn to speak English. He acknowledged that the "catch up year," plus the fact that these children must work, slows their education drastically.

Guerra said, "Migrant families depend upon the number of hands they have working. They must work to live. I can only admire these youngsters and their families; even though such work patterns hurt the children, they are not asking for handouts."

Guerra felt the special migrant education effort, financed by a $600,000 annual federal grant, was doing a good job.

I asked Alfonso Ramirez for his opinion.

He said, "In the middle grades, there hasn't been a significant change, even in Pharr. In the early grades they are getting better in the oral language approach and in the use of Spanish in instruction. But that is not helping the child who is already 11 or 12."

Those who are critical of the schools in the Rio Grande Valley—especially the 6-month migrant classes—say 80 percent of the students drop out.

I asked Ramirez about the dropout rate.

He answered the question with a question: "How would you feel if life was as frustrating as theirs? If you were a spectator in the classroom, if everything you were taught was difficult, if none of it felt good, if you were always behind, if they were always wanting you to hurry up, if they were always pushing you?"

He explained there.is tremendous pressure on these youngsters; the teachers are judged on how well the students perform. "They push so the kid is in the right book for the right grade.

The system is more concerned with the record and with having the children doing more than they can. There are great numbers of people who believe that if a non-English-speaking child begins school at age 6, by the third grade he ought to be at grade level, completely ignoring the fact he must learn a second language and he hasn't had the time."

"They really expect the kids to learn the language and at the same time keep up with the normal class and that is really quite impossible. Then in the fifth grade they are spectators, their reaction is to drop out as soon as they can.

"Many are uncomfortable because the school does not allow them to develop a personality that is pleasing to themselves. The child sees resentment in the school, from the principal, from the teacher, from other students. He knows he is in alien territory," Ramirez said, adding, "The parents are willing for the child to drop out. He is an economic asset in the fields, so the child quits school."

Ramirez and others are working on a bilingual instructional "package" the migrant child can take from school to school. It is part of a $51 million federal effort to reach these children with an educational program that develops some consistency.

Vidal A. Rivera, chief of the migrant education programs for the U.S. Office of Education, wrote: "In order to effect a significant program of assistance to the migrant worker and his children, the approach must be national. In the area of education, a national approach means interstate cooperation—an exchange of ideas, curriculum approaches, and methodology."[2]

The first steps were made in 1967 when Congress appropriated $9.7 million through the Elementary and Secondary Education Act for migrant education. Yearly this appropriation has increased until in 1970 it reached $51 million.

The 46 participating states and the federal government have established a centralized computer record-keeping system. The computer, located in Little Rock, had the academic and health records of 291,000 children stored in its migrant education memory banks at the end of the 1971–72 school year. When a child moves from one school district to another because his parents must move to find work, he or she is classified a migrant, even if the move is within the same county or state.

The old school—if it is participating in the computer program—sends the child's records to Little Rock. When the child enrolls in the new school, school officials teletype a request to the computer. Information vital to enrollment, such as grade placement and health inoculation records are teletyped back immediately. The more detailed records are mailed.

The problem with the total migrant education program is that it can be no better or no worse than the local school administrators who are in charge. The federal funds are granted to local authority.

Cassandra Stockburger, director of the National Committee on the Education of Migrant Children (NCEMC) said, "We regret to add yet another to a growing list of accounts of the failures in the public schools. This one is, perhaps, even sadder because migrant children have already been more shortchanged than any other among our nation's children."

Her words were part of a foreword to a detailed NCEMC report evaluating the U.S. Office of Education migrant programs throughout the nation.[3] The study was funded by the Ford Foundation and conducted by a dozen top educators. In the end the NCEMC concluded, "Solutions to the education problems of migrant children are not to be found in the hit-or-miss manner of present patterns of program development by the states and local school districts . . . ."

The NCEMC reported the existence of federal funding for migrant education "has brought about unprecedented involvement of the public schools"; it acknowledged that the USOE migrant programs branch was underfunded and therefore limited in what it could do; it also attacked the parent Department of Health, Education, and Welfare for squandering migrant education funds on studies that were not "specifically designed to further the cause of migrant children's education."

The problem with migrant education begins with the local schools' inability to reach most migrant children, or to even agree who is migrant and who is not. Some schools mix the migrant children with nonmigrant children of the same socio-economic-ethnic backgrounds. These classes are a blend of the children of the labor camps, the poor neighborhoods, the ghettos and colonias. Other schools segregate the migrants.

But either way administrators agree they are reaching only a small percent of the children and then only for short periods of time. In California, the chief of migrant programs, Leo Lopez, estimated 40,000 school-age migrant children were invisible to all government record-keeping programs. They are presumed to be working or babysitting or not going to school for other reasons.

How is this possible? Manteca and Lodi are located in the heart of California's San Joaquin Valley. The land is rich and crops grow abundantly most of the year. Manteca truant officer Dan Schneck said that in the fall, after schools have started, "There are literally hundreds of children working in the tomatoes. They are picking greens [fresh market fruit that ripens in transit]. They have no work permits. The schools are in session. I got the names of the growers, the labor contractors and their numbers and I took it to the labor commissioner and do you know what he asked for? He wanted me to go back and get the parents' names. Jesus, that's impossible. Each time I went to the labor commissioner, they asked me for more information.

"What I wish they would do is start nailing some of these growers. If the growers told the labor contractors who is allowed in the field, if they made it very plain no school-aged children were to be in their fields, or kids without work permits, then the contractors would see that it didn't happen.

"But they don't give a damn. All they care about is getting their crop in." In the end Schneck finally started threatening the parents, telling them he would go to the district attorney's office and seek complaints if they didn't put their children in school. Attendance improved.

Lodi schools' truant officer Raymond Quesada talked about the spring cherry harvest. In the spring, before schools are out, thousands of "ladder workers," the fruit pickers who follow the cherries, pears, apples, and other deciduous fruit crops, move into the Stockton-Lodi-Linden areas. Because of a severe housing shortage the pickers come two and three weeks early to find some place to live. Scores of families end up camping along the river banks and in the dry riverbeds. According to Quesada many of these families simply refuse to send their children to school. These are Anglo workers, primarily. Many live in the southern parts of the San Joaquin Valley, wintering in the olive and citrus harvests. Some come in from Arkansas and Oklahoma.

Quesada said, "Last year, I found a big camp where 52 kids weren't in school. They were from 12 families that had come in early, found a place to stay, but they were broke. The kids didn't have anything to wear to school and damn little to eat."

In the San Joaquin Valley—and in other farm areas across the nation—enforcement of the law is both difficult and, in the eyes of the labor law enforcement officers, futile, because conservative justice court judges openly state they feel children should learn to work.

Truant Officer Schneck informed labor law investigators of the violations he observed, citations were issued, and the cases were taken to court. After lengthy postponements some ended in small fines or probation.

One judge bawled out the lawmen for picking on a family that was trying to stay off welfare by working the children—even though school was in session.

Often the school systems are bent to help the farmer. In Maine, schools are recessed for the potato harvest. In Oregon, the school children are recruited by the state. In Louisiana, at strawberry harvest time, Ponchatoula officials didn't start the federally funded migrant school until after lunch so the children could get in five or six hours of work before going to classes. A special migrant education program bused 150 children to an abandoned school that had been used by Black students before integration closed it down.

Cassandra Stockburger charged the program was both a violation of the Civil Rights Act—because the program segregated migrants—and a violation of the Fair Labor Standards Act provisions against employing children 16 and under while school is in session. The U.S. Labor Department's child labor watchdogs agreed, but explained they had not pursued the matter because "some education was better than none."

In a taped interview with Ms. Stockburger in 1971, Louisiana Migrant Education Director William Junkin agreed, "What we've got going is kind of a dodge. . . . There is a certain type of segregation taking place. It makes a long day . . . [but] our state commissioner of labor says there is no violation. He says they [the children] are working for their parents. We operate [migrant] school from noon until six in the evening. We bring them in and give them lunch after they finish working. . . . It's the only thing we can do and still do some good for the children."

The willingness of some agri-business-oriented school administrators to accommodate child labor on the farm is not confined to any one geographic area. One Florida county coordinator for migrant education said the compulsory attendance law was not rigidly enforced. He claims he tries to keep a "liberal" view and asks his field staff not to be "hard-nosed" about the regulations.

He said, "If there is sufficient evidence that the children are really needed to help earn enough money to support the family we sort of let them slide. After all we want to encourage people to assume responsibility for themselves and members of their families, rather than having them sitting around waiting for a handout."[4]

In one Florida junior high school the absence rate of Black students ran about one-third daily, or about 190 absentees a week. The Black assistant principal reported about 150 of these absentees were working with their parents in agriculture.[5]

In Ohio's fall tomato harvest it took federal officers four years of concerted effort to get the children out of the fields when school started. The effort was led by Federal Wage and Hour Area Supervisor Robert Pietrykowski, and success came only after the officers discovered the key was economics, not education.

As in most farming areas where child labor was found, the Ohio tomato growers insisted they did not want the children in their fields. They claimed there was no way to keep them out of the fields. The parents wanted the children to work.

The migrant parents complained the schools refused to take the children, or if they did take them the Ohio school work was not recognized by the schools in Texas or Florida. One Florida mother indignantly told me, "We don't put our kids in those Ohio schools because the teachers there put 'em back a year. If my boy is in the fourth grade here, they puts him in the third grade in Ohio."

While some Ohio schools try hard to assimilate the migrant population—and the job is a tough one because of the extra staffing and extra space needed for only four or five weeks —other Ohio schools resist.

One Ohio farmer discovered how the schools in his area rejected migrants when he insisted the children of his workers go to school. The school bus driver had different ideas.

The farmer explained, "When them kids got on that bus, the driver told them there wasn't no place to sit, and they had to stand. I didn't know it for a long time and when I found out I asked [the father of the children] why didn't he come to me before. There is a state law that no child is to stand in a school bus anytime.

"I think this was a racial deal. Anyway, we got it straightened out and they went on the bus after that, but when they got to school, all they got was a piece of paper four inches wide and eight inches long and one little stub of a pencil and there they sat, in school, all day long. Our schools don't want to bother with them."

More Ohio schools are "bothering" with migrants now because of Pietrykowski's four-year anti-child-labor campaign. The number of violations of the Fair Labor Standards Act dropped from 340 in 1970 to 46 cases in 1971.

How was it done?

Pietrykowski started with the farmers, heard their story, and then went to the schools. The school superintendents complained that they did not have the staff or the space for such a short period of instruction. Pietrykowski tried to convince them that they should plan for the September through October "bulge" in enrollment, only to have the school administrators switch themes: the parents refused to send the children.

The attendance officers told Pietrykowski they would like to enforce the law, but they were too shorthanded to meet the task he asked of them. Pietrykowski went back to the school administrators and got them to hire extra truant officers for the fall months. But then the attendance officers complained the local judges would not support their law and order efforts.

Pietrykowski talked to the judges, and they agreed to cooperate. By this time Pietrykowski and his staff were getting a bit short-tempered. The Ohio statistics for four years were topping the nation in child labor law violations, but there was little sign anyone was taking such violations seriously. Pietrykowski switched tactics. The Fair Labor Standards Act has a provision that allows a federal court to block the interstate shipment of products produced by the illegal labor of children.

Most of Ohio's tomato crop goes into juice, catsup, and other products processed by the large canning corporations.

Pietrykowski told the processors about the "hot cargo" provisions in the Act. "It means that if a canner accepts tomatoes from a farmer who has harvested his crop by working underage children, the canner can be enjoined from shipping his product in interstate commerce for a period of at least thirty days."

The farmers got the message, via their new contracts with canners. If they violated the law, the contracts were void. Although the crackdown doesn't ensure that children will be in school, it makes it a lot tougher for them to work in the fields.

Without the work of the children the family suffers, yet if the children do work there is no time for the education they must have if they are to break out of the vicious poverty cycle. A few, like Ricardo and Juan, do make it, but they are the exceptions.

Juan, the younger brother, told how he began the first grade in Ohio, as the family worked in the tomato harvest. On the day school opened the parents went to work early as usual, leaving the older children to get all the kids ready for school. Ricardo—who had been enrolled the first time by his older sister—was to enroll Juan.

Ricardo recalls, "Juan was real scared, but I told him it was all right. We went in the office and just sat down and waited. When they see you, they know why you are there.

"Pretty soon a lady would take you to her desk and she would ask you a whole bunch of questions. They would always ask how long you were going to be there, and you'd always give them some kind of estimate.

"I guess that is one of the reasons why a lot of the teachers didn't care too much about you. They would be talking to themselves and you'd hear them say, 'He's only going to be here a month or three weeks,' like that," Ricardo said.

Ricardo took Juan to the first-grade class, instructing him to find a seat in the back part of the room, to go to it and sit down and be quiet.

Juan said, "I was really scared. I sat there, but I didn't know what was happening. The teacher asked me a question but I couldn't understand her. She would say my name, then some words. I was so scared, I just started crying. Ricardo was in the third grade then, I think. Anyway the teacher, she couldn't get me to stop crying, so she took me to him.

"From then on, I spent my time in the third grade. When they would take me to the first grade, I would cry, so they left me in Ricardo's room. It was fine until they told my parents," Juan laughed now.

The parents were very serious about their children's education, but rather than punish their youngest son, they promised to buy him a bicycle if he would do as the school officials ordered. "And that's what they did. They bought me a bicycle and we had to go hungry for a few meals."

Ricardo, Juan, and their brothers and sisters started school each fall in Ohio. When the tomato harvest was finished the family moved to the wine grapes in Michigan, and the children spent a month in Michigan schools. From the wine grapes they made the long drive into west Texas, into the cotton harvest.

Ricardo recalled, "We just had a new truck, we needed more space and my father bought this pickup truck. We were coming from Ohio to Texas and we had this accident. There was a car coming at us and the driver was stone drunk. We weren't hurt, but we had to spend a week in that town. They put us up in a barn, and we had to stay in that barn. They gave us some state food, and all, but I don't think they wanted us to stay."

The feeling of ethnic rejection is strong within the two

brothers, there is still a trace of bitterness as they talk about the schools they attend.

Juan: "The schools have given in to the system, to what the white educational system is supposed to be like. If we want to make it, we have to do it their [Anglo middle-class] way, you know?"

Ricardo cut in, "But we Chicanos will never make it that way. We can't. And I don't blame the young Chicanos right now, for not being able to make it, not after they been away [migrating] for five or six months. When you come in late, it really messes you up.

"For instance, when school starts, the class goes right into math, right? And I was always missing out, you know? It is essential to get the fundamentals, but you come in and they are already in the second or third week. It's only basic math, but even then, I was two or three weeks, then two or three months, behind.

"So you fall behind, year after year, term after term, so you start getting lost, start getting discouraged, and then you have this thing about being afraid. I got lost and I was afraid and I didn't have any sense of pride, of who I was, so in the eighth grade, I dropped out."

As Ricardo and Juan talked, we were standing beside their car on a shady side street in a small town in Oregon's Willamette Valley. Across the street, in a supermarket parking lot, the local Chicano high school students pulled in, parked their cars, talked, horsed around, got back in their cars and drove slowly around, only to circle back again and park. It was Sunday afternoon and most of them were dressed in clean jeans, well-pressed shirts.

They were the sons and daughters of migrants who had settled here, they worked in the berries and beans when school was not in session. They were a minority here, but their numbers were growing. So was their anxiety, their suspicion of Anglos.

There were no Chicano teachers, no Chicano counselors in the schools to advise them. Ricardo and Juan, both students in a Pacific Northwest University, came into towns like this on weekends to talk to these high schoolers, to encourage them to stay in school and organize themselves, and to demand that their educational needs be met—via bilingual teachers, and a cultural and historic content that honestly reflects the Spanish-speaking influences on the western United States.

Ricardo explained, "There is nothing in the schools we attended—and the schools they attended [he waved out toward the passing parade]—that pertained to us. Language was always a problem, sure, but it was more than that. There was no cultural understanding. They couldn't reach us because they didn't know us.

"They [the teachers] would pat us on the head and say, 'You are cute' but that isn't what we wanted, we wanted understanding. We wanted a sense of pride, but there was nothing we could fall back on to say we were proud of.

"The schools didn't have a damn thing set up for us as Chicanos or as migrants . . . you were always being called 'dumb.' The Anglo kids would call you 'dumb Mexicans.' There wasn't anything we could defend ourselves with, so we got this little plot [of ground] to ourselves."

The brothers described how the young Chicanos would take over one corner of the school ground and would herd up protectively. Trespassers were not tolerated. The Chicanos would fight the gabachos, the gringos, the Anglos if need be to protect their land, their identity.

The history books they read had no accurate portrayal of Mexican-American history. Juan explained, "You know the things they say about Mexican heroes, they always put them down. Even now, I am taking a course at the university and in it they have Zapata and Poncho Villa as bandits. In the picture they identify them as the 'Revolutionary Bandits of Mexico.' That is not true. They were great men.

"At home our parents, especially my father, he says we should tell our professors to go read the true history of Mexico, to look at what Francisco Villa did for Mexico, to study the life of Emiliano Zapata."

The parents of Ricardo and Juan are strong, determined people. They insisted their children stay in school, they gave them a sense of pride in their ethnic and cultural background. But even this was almost not enough. Ricardo dropped out in the eighth grade, to work in the fields.

He explained, "They [teachers and administrators] take away your pride. You have to assimilate, and you know it. That is how, that is where the mind gets mixed up. You try to do it the gabacho way, but you still have your parents. And where do you go? Sometimes you hide between the gabacho and the Chicano. That is what happened to me.

"In school, especially in elementary school, I would forget my parents for a while, then when I came home, I saw what we were going through and I didn't know what to do."

This sharp contrast between the middle-class world of schools and the poverty of farm workers' home lives is one of the constant themes running through the conversations I had with young Blacks and Chicanos all across the nation.

One high school boy in California, the student body president in a school dominated by Anglos, broke into tears as we talked. He was strung out between the two worlds. His parents pressured him to deny his Mexicanness and to imitate the middle-class Anglo. He did. He was singled out as a "good Mexican" and asked to speak at the Kiwanis and Rotary Clubs.

He realized he was a symbol used by the Anglo society to prove assimilation was possible. The Chicano students labeled him a coconut, a Tio Taco, a youth who was brown on the outside, but white on the inside, an Uncle Tom.

What turned Ricardo and Juan on to college?

Ricardo answered first: "When I went into the service [Army], I didn't have my GED [General Education Development] diploma. I had to work twice as hard in the Army just to prove I could do it, so when I got out, I said I'll get my GED and I'll get me a job, because that is what the system calls for.

"But then I saw myself sweeping floors, working in the department stores, and I asked myself if that is what I want to do the rest of my life.

"I didn't want it that way and a friend of mine who had his GED was in the Chicano movement and he put me onto the HEP thing."

HEP stands for High School Equivalency Program, a federally funded migrant education project to get youngsters like Ricardo prepared to take the GED tests that, if passed, substitute for a high school diploma. There are HEP classes located all along the migrant routes.

Ricardo enrolled at El Paso. He said, "Our instructors made us proud of ourselves. That was the main thing. We got it through our heads that we could do it.

"We had an Anglo math teacher and he worked hard with us. At first I didn't trust him. He wanted to help and, well, the rest of the Chicanos seemed to trust him, so I said okay, and I really tried.

"They gave us a lot of counseling, and they were talking about college and telling me how I had the GI Bill and that would help pay for my college. I thought it was impossible. Nobody had ever talked about college to me, and I never even dreamed I would go, I didn't even know what it was. But, I tried, you know?"

Juan's route was somewhat easier because he had an older brother who had already tested the problems he faced. Juan said, "To go to college I thought you had to be under the books all the time, that you had to be very, very smart, that you had to be a genius or something. I didn't want to go to college, I wanted to join the Marines, I thought that was better.

"Since they [high school counselors] tell you you have to

have so much of an average [grade] and that you have to take so many tests and get such good scores, I didn't want to go to college. But two girls [members of the Chicano movement] came and talked to me, several times. They brought me applications. I took some tests—I found out I got a 1.05 [low D] on those tests, but it didn't matter, they still let me in.''

When we talked, Juan was going into his junior year with a 3.5 grade point average. On the letter scale that is halfway between A and B and he was a bit miffed. "I should have had a 3.7, but I goofed off too much." His brother, Ricardo, is making a 2.8 grade point. Studying for him is more difficult.

Throughout the West, there is unrest among Chicano students. There are a half-dozen or more Chicano student organizations; some are fiery, some quietly reserved, most develop individualized causes geared to meet specific problems—but at the root of all of them is this developing ethnic-cultural pride. Young Chicanos will point out that as the Mayflower dropped its anchor off Plymouth Rock there was an established university in Mexico City, that before the Spaniards developed St. Augustine, Florida—the oldest European colony in the United States—there were great civilizations in Mexico. Centuries before Daniel Boone built a log fort in Kentucky, the Mayas of Mexico invented the abstract symbol of zero to simplify mathematics and they had developed a calendar that was more efficient than that of their European conquerors.

Such thoughts and the romanticizing of their cultural-historical background are important to the young Chicanos. They want the school to include their culture, they want Chicano teachers, Chicano counselors. In short, they want understanding.

In some parts of the country, school officials feel the growing pressures from the militant young Chicanos and efforts are being made to understand what it is they are trying to say.

A group of rural California high school counselors gathered in a workshop to discuss dropout problems and learn more about the Mexican-American students. For them, the word "Chicano" was still not quite acceptable.

To help them understand the Mexican-American students, the group invited the Teatro Campesino, directed by Luis Valdez, to give some interpretative performances. Valdez, formerly with Cesar Chavez and the farm workers' union, is the creator of the Teatro, the Workers' Theater. The Teatro, under Valdez, has made a national reputation with its broad, stinging parodies and heavy satire that exaggerate the already gross inequities suffered by workers in the field.

For the counselors, Valdez and his actors improvised several "actos" (acts) portraying Chicano students in conflict with the system. One of the central themes involved a high school boy's love of school in conflict with the economic need of his family. His father was ailing and the boy had to work in the fields. His school work suffered. He was absent when school regulations required that he be in class.

As he fell behind his counselor argued that his need for an education should keep him in school. The themes of the playlets were—by Teatro standards—understated. Valdez was being as gentle on his audience as he could, and still present the Chicano student view. The actors were young adults who were working out their own story.

Afterwards the administrators and counselors gave the actos only polite applause, and then only because tradition demanded it and because silence would have been more embarrassing. Valdez asked if there were questions. There was no response.

The Anglo audience was either offended or puzzled. They knew the system and what it demanded of students and teachers alike and they were here to learn from Valdez and the Teatro what they, as counselors, could do to help mold the Mexican-American student into that system.

The actos had suggested the system itself needed to be reshaped to meet student needs. That was a disturbing thought.

One woman, a nice person who has demonstrated over the years that she wants to help students blend into American society, was the only counselor with enough gumption and candor to speak her mind.

She told Valdez his actos were offensive and unrealistic and because of this she had become angry and had stopped listening. This troubled her, for she had come to find answers, not to be criticized in this abrasive manner. Her candor gave Valdez pause. He is normally enigmatic, mercurial, cocky. He has a sharp wit and his anger and laughter always bubble close to the surface.

The question—or rather the statement—brought him to a stop. He wanted to breach the gap, to make her understand what it was they were trying to say. He tried and failed. The distance between them was too great. He was the voice of the farm worker, she the wife of a farmer. He was an outsider, a disturbing, abrasive, brown man, she a middle-class high school counselor in a system that does not tolerate disturbance.

Another counselor broke the impasse by asking a comfortable question: What does the word Chicano mean?

Valdez switched gears, he was back in his cocky, bouncy stride again. Using his cigar for effect, he began a definition that can last twenty minutes or two hours, depending upon the length of the history lesson that goes with it.

The explanation delves into culture and into linguistics. The language of Mexico is a blend of the Nahuatl, the tongue of the Aztec, and of Spanish. Before the Spanish conquests, the *X* had the sound of *Ch* and therefore Mexican is pronounced Me-chi-ca-no. For Valdez it is but a short step to Chicano, the word that is used to blend all that is ethnic, all that is cultural, and all that is historic, from the deserts of Baja, California, to the forests of Quintana Roo.

But the point of the counselors' conference got lost in the worries of ethnic confrontation. The subject was supposed to be the discovery of ways to keep minority students in school so they could begin to learn the basic skills needed to take them out of the fields of poverty.

If education cannot do that—and by and large it has not—then the black and the brown students who drop out are demonstrating more logic than the school administrators who seek to make them sit in class. If, after these youngsters stay in school for 12 or 13 years, they must return to Belle Glade and go each morning to the Loading Ramp to find work harvesting winter vegetables, what is the point of school?

The $51 million federal migrant education program by design is trying to take education to the children as they migrate. Special emphasis is being placed on bilingual instruction, on field trips and programs to broaden the childrens' viewpoint.

Programs like HEP are attracting dropouts and some are going on to college. But, if the migrant education programs are measured in terms of the total numbers of migrant students enrolled in junior high and high school, they are failing.

After the fifth and sixth grades the enrollment figures drop drastically. When the National Committee on the Education of Migrant Children went over the records of 35,000 migrant children in 1968–69 programs, it found only 201 graduating high school seniors. And these were in 28 of the 120 projects studied. The remaining three-quarters of the projects had no high school graduates.[6]

The NCEMC asked the 28 districts what each had done to keep students in school until they graduated. Factors listed included: part-time jobs; college scholarships; individual help from teachers; individualized curricula and special courses, including language arts, industrial arts, home and family living, and vocational programs; participation in athletics and other extracurricular activities; intensive counseling of pupils and parents; supportive services for students and families, including clothing, shoes, better housing and health care, and care for younger brothers and sisters so that high school students would not have to leave school to babysit.[7]

These schools did not bend the rules so the children could work in the fields, they did not tailor the program so the farmers' crops were harvested first. Such schools developed full, expensive programs.

More of this type of programming is possible without increasing the Congressionally approved level of spending. The NCEMC study of 1968–69 budgets revealed migrant educational administrators failed to spend $17 million that had been appropriated for education. In addition, migrant school administrators failed to spend $954,000 budgeted for food services and $686,000 budgeted for health care, despite the fact that hunger and malnutrition and resulting poor health are the most critical problems faced by migrant children.

But even if all the hungry children were fed, and educational programs were developed with the unspent funds, there are those who question the wisdom of government programs supporting the continued migration patterns.

Dr. Robert Coles, the Harvard Medical School child psychiatrist who spent a decade studying migrant children, said, ''I think all of the efforts we are making—and they are meager compared to what they should be along the lines of migrant health, migrant education, and even the inclusion of some migrants under minimum-wage laws—is not going to finally help these children.

''The efforts may at times provide them with some minimal health services and they certainly need them as they are not getting them. It may help their education, to some extent. But as long as these children are carried around from one part of the country to the next, we are never going to solve the problem of the damage done to these children.

''So I would unequivocally say that we are going in the wrong direction by trying to deliver certain minimal health and educational services to them, even economic services, so long as these children are living this kind of uprooted life.

"I think we have got to stop these families from moving the way they do. Now this has been shown not only by me. Anyone who reads *The Grapes of Wrath* will understand that implicit in the life of these people is not only poverty, but rootlessness and migrancy itself.

"I think the Federal Government should stop supporting migrancy as a way of life, for instance as the Department of Labor does. Why should the American taxpayers be putting money into something that is so destructive to the minds of American children?"[8]

7

How would you like it if we gave a child a free lunch and then found his father out drinking in a bar?

—A rural school official

Hunger: Knock on Any Door

In 1939 Secretary of Agriculture Henry Wallace instituted a radical poverty program—the distribution of farm surplus commodities free to the poor—and declared: "The day is not far distant when all the people in the United States will be adequately nourished . . . ."

In 1946 Congress passed the National School Lunch Act and, recognizing the poor could not afford to participate, made special provisions for free or reduced-price lunches for "all children who are . . . unable to pay the full cost."

In the 1950's the school milk program was passed to improve the youthful health of the nation; in the 1960's Lyndon Johnson declared war on all poverty and Congress passed the Child Nutrition Act.

Clearly a national concern for the health and welfare of the poor was being expressed through such legislative actions. Yet thirty years and five administrations after Henry Wallace made his prediction, a series of public and private inquiries revealed that millions of men, women, and children were hungry, malnourished, starving. Such descriptive words brought howls of conservative protest. How could there be shortages of food in a land so rich? Where was the evidence? There were no starving beggar children in the streets, no skeletal bodies lying in the gutters. The idea of *starvation* was rejected out of hand; *hunger* was judged too strong a word; if there was *malnutrition* it was caused by ignorance and poor diet, not lack of income.

The rhetoric of poverty politics became familiar, the patterns of actions obvious. Conservatives and liberals argued. Congress appropriated millions, and great bureaus were structured to distribute the national largess. But such assistance was grudgingly given and final control was left in the hands of local politicians. While the great welfare machinery grew more ponderous, federal food programs were administered more as economic levers to prop up the sagging farm market prices than as sustenance for the poor.

Welfare has become the farmers' unemployment insurance program. Farm wages are so low and work so sporadic, a seasonal laborer cannot make a living, even with the help of his wife and children. In liberal welfare states like California these "underemployed" and unemployed farm workers have been given assistance, if they got through the application process and survived the security checks. (One zealous welfare department had the district attorney administering lie-detector tests to see if those on aid were honest in reporting their income.) In many of the farming areas of the nation welfare is little more than a sustenance, and for years migrants have been denied even this meager bit of aid because they were not residents of the county or state.

The welfare system, as it is run by the bureaucrats and manipulated by farm politics, evokes a special kind of bitterness in men like Jesús Gonzales. When a man's children are hungry, when there is no food in the house and no work is available anywhere, it is difficult to understand "the welfare lady" explaining why she is rejecting his plea for help.

Jesús Gonzales, his wife, and their 10 children live in a small, two-bedroom frame house out in the country. The house is old, but comfortable, in a crowded way. The indoor plumbing works, a rusty squirrel-cage cooler hangs in the front-room window blowing cool air into the house on hot summer days. Out in front there's a small patch of Bermuda grass where the children can play without getting dirty and where it is pleasant to sit on summer evenings and look across the flat California farmland.

The house is a rental—it costs $100 a month—but it has been home for several years, the first real home the family has ever had. Off in the distance, Jesús points to a tall water tower that stands over the town where his children go to school. Main Street is only four blocks long, lined with one-story, false-front stores and shops. There are half a dozen service stations, a couple of farm machinery dealerships, a justice court and the school.

In the middle of the town there is a two-story brick building, an 80-year-old structure that houses the local bank and, upstairs, the offices of an accountant and an attorney. The town's principal business is agriculture. Old warehouse-like packing sheds line the railroad tracks that parallel Main Street. The managers of these sheds, the businessmen, and the service employees of the community live on quiet, tree-shaded streets, all within walking distance of "downtown."

Out beyond these residential areas there are the shantytowns of Black farm workers and the barrios where Spanish-speaking farm workers live. Jesús and his family moved into the area as migrant farm workers from Texas. They wanted to settle, buy a big truck and trailer, and Jesús would contract to haul hay and sugar beets. First, they had to earn the down payment. The entire family worked. Even the smallest youngsters went into the orchards and vineyards. The little ones ran errands, fetching a water bottle, a bucket, picking a little fruit. When the grape harvest was finished, in the late fall, the children were registered in school.

Jesús recalled, "We were living in a little old shack then, it had only two rooms and the floors sagged when you moved. We got our water from a faucet right there by the big water tower. We hauled it in those 5-gallon milk cans. We would cover the cans with old sacks to try to keep the water cool, but it wasn't any use. The sun always made the cans hot, and the water never tasted good," he said.

The first season had been a good one, Jesús found work through the winter, doing odd jobs, driving tractors, or repairing equipment. Three ranchers in the area kept him almost steadily employed. When work was available, the children would go out with their mother on weekends.

It took three years to save enough to pay down on a $2,500 used truck and trailer. Licenses for the truck and trailer cost Jesús $950 a year. But even with such extra costs his profits from hauling hay and sugar beets are greater than the wages he earns as a farm worker.

When I met Jesús he still owed $600 on the truck, and the family was in desperate financial shape. It was late spring and normally Jesús would have been well into his hauling season, but it had been raining hard all winter and spring. Growers could not work the fields. The hay crops were late.

As we talked, Jesús walked around his truck, inspecting the load of baled hay, tightening down the ropes. It was the first load of the season. He was sweating, his head and shoulders were covered with hay dust and chaff. The leather apron he wore was blackened with use. The truck was parked in front of his house in the country. Three of his smaller children had climbed up in the truck's cab and were playing truck driver.

Jesús was angry: "They [the welfare department] made me feel like a bum, but I'm not a bum. I'm a citizen. I pay taxes. All I wanted was a little help to pay my bills and to get something to eat for my kids, just until I was working again. But the welfare lady said, 'no.' ''

Like most farm workers—even those with a truck—Jesús Gonzales and his family live on the brink of financial disaster. If their income stops—as it did that winter—they are in trouble. Even the odd jobs he usually did around the three farms at that time of year dwindled into nothing. Jesús had established credit at a nearby country grocery store and gas station. He charged most of the groceries, and had stalled most of his creditors so that he had been able to make partial payments on the truck.

School lunches cost the family $40 a month. Most of the time there had been enough food in the house to get by, a bag of beans, some flour for tortillas, some chili. Finally there was no money for school lunches. The children were going to school on a breakfast of beans and coffee and, because they could not pay for lunch anymore, they went outside and walked around the school grounds at noon.

The rains continued to pour out of the gray sky, the land was soggy, and great puddles surrounded the Gonzales house. The children all had runny noses, they coughed and didn't feel well.

The final blow came late in January, when the grocery store owner said he could no longer extend them credit. The store owner was carrying dozens of other families with large bills. He was sorry, but he had to have cash to continue in business himself.

Jesús said, ''We had been hungry before, but never like this. Maybe if we weren't trying so hard to keep the truck payments going we could have squeezed by. But we couldn't, and I had to borrow more to pay the license so I could be ready for work.''

When things were the bleakest, Jesús Gonzales swallowed his pride and drove 35 miles into the county seat, to the welfare department. He needed help and, while the welfare department had a bad reputation among the people he knew, it was the only place for him to turn. Afterward he wished he had not gone, and he vowed he would never go back.

What happened?

"The welfare lady listened to me, she let me tell her the whole problem. Then she helped me fill out all these papers. Then she shook her head, said she was sorry that I was not eligible."

Why?

He owned a $1,900 equity in the truck and trailer. No one with over $1,500 in personal property is eligible for welfare. Jesús Gonzales asked, "What the hell did they want from me? Am I supposed to sell my truck and go on welfare forever? Shit!"

The rejection was not absolute. The county welfare department gave the Gonzales family a box of groceries, surplus commodities the U.S. Department of Agriculture purchases from the nation's farmers and then distributes to the counties that elect to participate in the program.

"They [welfare commissary officials] said the box was for the family for one month. I'm not going to complain about that food, but it lasted only 16 days. We were told we couldn't get more until next month, so we went hungry again.

"I did send a note to school, asking them please to feed the kids. I promised to pay them back later so the kids could at least get one meal a day," he said. The school granted the Gonzales children the credit.

While the winter had been hard and had left the family deep in debt, they considered themselves lucky. They had survived. None of the family had been critically ill, no one had been hurt bad enough to require a doctor.

Not everyone is this lucky. For most farm workers, winter is a time of hunger and privation, of sickness and death. In the spring there is life and work and food, in the summer the harvests mean work for everyone, and some money can be saved. The fall is a time of extra hard work, to store up enough reserve to make it through the winter.

Winter is the critical time. In California's Fresno County, a pediatrician in the county-operated general hospital reported seven malnourished infants had been admitted in early spring of 1969. Officially the diagnosis was "failure to thrive." These seven cases were in addition to the routine pneumonias and other admissions where malnourishment might be a contributing factor.

The pediatrician explained, "This time of year we see a lot of anemias, low-grade anemias. You get the picture of a pale, fat baby, behind in development, sometimes irritable, subject to frequent infections and prolonged colds. Growth charts show the poor and underfed are smaller, the youngsters are slowed down. And there is some evidence malnutrition, this long-term, low-grade stuff, may have some effect on a child's mental development."

In nearby Kings County, where individual corporate cotton and grain farmers receive up to $4 million each in federal subsidies, a study of 250 farm worker preschool-age children revealed 49 percent suffered from "functional anemia," an indication of protein-and-vitamin-deficient diets and possible malnutrition. This Corcoran City school survey also established a relationship between hunger and family income: the poorer the farm worker family, the more malnourished the children.

In Colorado, Dr. Peter Chase, a pediatrician teaching at the University of Colorado medical school, studied 300 migrant children from 151 families. Clinical tests revealed various signs of serious malnutrition, including evidence of growth retardation, rickets, and marasmus.[1] One or two children showed early symptoms of kwashiorkor, a gross form of malnutrition normally seen only in the most underdeveloped nations.

Dr. Chase reported these seasonal farm worker families suffered an infant mortality rate three times the national average; half their children had never been immunized against diphtheria, pertussis, tetanus, or polio; 10 percent had never seen a doctor. Fifty percent of the children had serious vitamin deficiencies and among this deficient group the doctor found more frequent skin and upper respiratory tract infections.

Most of these families come from south Texas. They live in the small towns and out in isolated colonias where medical help of any kind is almost nonexistent. In Hidalgo County, Texas, home of 37,000 migrant farm worker families, there are 4,000 patients for each doctor; in Starr County, the ratio is 10,000 to 1. In Willacy County, there is no hospital.[2]

In McAllen, Dr. Ramiro Casso said, "There is a lot of illness, a lot of disease in [Hidalgo] County. It is out there, hidden in the colonias and barrios. The people are too proud to come in and beg, and they have a pretty good idea they are going to be turned down anyway. The problems are lack of adequate medical care for the general [farm worker] population, the lack of hospital facilities. I don't mean lack of physical facilities so much as I mean lack of accessibility to such facilities."

Dr. Casso is an open, easily met man, who has practiced medicine in the Rio Grande Valley for nearly two decades. His graying hair and square-set, substantial appearance give him a fatherly look that is not at all in keeping with his reputation as an abrasive, outspoken critic of agri-business farm labor practices, malnutrition, and lack of medical care for the poor. But Dr. Casso does far more than talk about such problems. During the summer he sees 50 patients a day in his well-equipped offices, in winter the number doubles.

Because too many farm workers could not afford any medical attention, Antonio Orendain of the United Farm Workers Union and Dr. Casso established a free clinic in the UFWU offices. Dr. Casso and a few others volunteered their services until public funds were found to hire a full-time physician.

I asked Dr. Casso what the Number One medical problem among farm workers was.

His answer: "Malnutrition. Protein malnutrition. It affects almost everybody. It shows up as anemias, nutritional anemias, the wasting of muscles, poor resistance to infections, increased incidents of a lot of things you and I don't have in our children, such as draining ears, upper respiratory infections, a lot of skin infections, diarrheas.

"If we could feed these people the protein they need, the medical problems would virtually be eliminated. But we have such potent enemies in the Department of Agriculture and the subcommittees of Congress. Well, to tell you how backward we are, we don't have a food stamp program in this county yet [1971]. We have to depend upon surplus commodities, and they are just what the name implies, surplus.

"These kids need an adequate protein supplement, the surplus food won't do it. The government surplus commodities are traditionally poor sources of protein and the programs don't provide fresh meats. A lot of migrant families don't eat meat but once every two or three weeks, their diet is beans and tortillas and that kind of thing. Beans have protein, but not all the essential amino acids you find in meat."

According to Dr. Casso the migrant may be better off than the farm worker who stays the year round in the Rio Grande Valley because by migrating the worker becomes part of a readily identifiable group and can receive emergency federal aid. Those who remain in one area and work are invisible to most, if not all, governmental functions and services. They suffer the same malnutrition and medical problems.

In South Carolina U.S. Senator Ernest F. Hollings toured the urban and rural areas of his home state and found hunger. "In Beaufort County, I visited a shack in which 16 persons lived and there was no light, no heat, no running water, hot or cold, no bath, no toilet. The entire store of food consisted of a slab of fatback, a half-filled jar of locally harvested oysters, and a stick of margarine.

"Dr. Kenneth Aycock, our state health official who was accompanying me, tentatively diagnosed a man in the house as suffering from pellegra, a disease supposedly nonexistent in this country. In the same house one small child had rickets, and another was recovering from scurvy.

"At another stop two of the children receive hot lunches at school by paying 35 cents a day. The cost of these children eating lunch is $14 [a month] out of a total family income of $40. When I pointed out that Congress had provided a free lunch program [a state official] said, 'Well, Senator, that hasn't trickled down this far yet. Maybe we are just too far down the coast, anyway, we haven't got it.' " (Authorization for the lunch program was passed by Congress in 1946.)

Senator Hollings continued, "At one house, four children were home from school so their mother could wash the only clothes they had. The children, they eat grits for breakfast, and greens or cabbage for supper when they have it." [3]

Local families like these work seasonally on nearby "truck farms" in crops like tomatoes, cucumbers and snap beans. But the problem, in places like Beaufort County, is under-employment. Most of the available work is on a dozen large farms, but only when the crops are ready for harvest. Even with a federal minimum wage guarantee of $1.30 an hour, parents cannot earn enough to keep food on the table and to clothe their children, because the work is so seasonal. They must find other work or apply for welfare assistance.

A team of health experts from the University of South Carolina examined 177 Beaufort County children. These were the children of the local poor, of the seasonal farm workers. Most of the children were shorter and weighed less than they should for their chronological ages. One child in four was anemic, with one in three having vitamin deficiencies. [4]

Dr. James P. Carter, a pediatrician and nutrition expert, said, "The most striking physical findings on these children were distended abdomens in 41 percent. This distention is most likely due to varying degrees of malabsorption, secondary to the presence of the intestinal roundworm, *Ascaris lumbricoides*.''

After reporting the various disorders found in the children—the list was similar to reports from Colorado or Texas or Florida—Dr. Carter concluded, "By and large the children would appear normal to a casual observer except for the distended abdomen. Yet significant numbers of them are seriously malnourished."[5]

The calorie intake of these children was one-half the recommended allowance. The three-to-six-year-olds were getting only 800 calories. Dr. Carter observed, "This caloric insufficiency is certainly not enough to support the patient and barely enough to support the worms."[6]

Of the 177 children examined, 98 had intenstinal worms. These worms are from 9 to 12 inches long and a child may have as many as 100 in his intestines. To reproduce, the male and female worms must be together in one child. The result of their mating produces two hundred thousand eggs that pass out of the child in the fecal material. If the child defecates promiscuously in the soil, the soil remains contaminated for up to a year.

A child playing in the dirt puts his hands in his mouth, swallowing the egg capsules containing the infective larvae. The eggs hatch, the larvae penetrates the intestine, and the bloodstream carries them to the liver and eventually to the lungs. There they grow, break out into the air sacs, ascend the windpipe (the trachea) and are swallowed again and develop to maturity in about 60 to 85 days.[7]

In the rural farm labor camps, in the shantytowns that spring up around the farming communities, in the ghettos and barrios in the major agri-business cities, there are often intolerable sanitary conditions. Decrepit housing, inadequate sewage and garbage disposal, rodents and insects—all contribute to the high incidence of disease.

In 1968 doctors in the Variety Children's Hospital in Miami examined 23 children of farm workers from the Immokalee area. The children were selected at random. Doctors found 38 clinical diseases, many of them traceable to malnutrition. There were 11 cases of iron deficiency anemias, 14 cases of upper respiratory infections, and two cases of pneumonia.

During the late 1960's such reports documenting hunger, malnutrition, and disease were little more than disturbing abstractions. Such problems were—and still are—tucked too far back in the boondocks to be readily observed.

But when CBS-TV documented Hunger-U.S.A. these problems came into full view. The official USDA reaction was one of wounded innocence. CBS was accused of distortion by Secretary of Agriculture Orville Freeman. The controversy over the news presentation sidetracked the main issue: hunger relief.

In 1969 President Richard Nixon's urban affairs advisor, Daniel Patrick Moynihan, wanted a firsthand report on hunger and the effectiveness of the federal food program. At the time he had two Army officers on his staff, men on loan from West Point. Moynihan asked Captain Terrence P. Goggin and Captain Clifford Hendrix to survey the federal food programs to see if the hungry were being fed.

The officers toured 15 counties in New York, Mississippi, Missouri, and California and reported back to the White House. Their report was not publicized. A year later amid charges that the report was being suppressed because it was too revealing, Senator George McGovern finally got the White House to agree that the two officers could testify before his Select Committee on Nutrition and Human Need.

On June 19, 1970, Captain Goggin and Captain Hendrix appeared before the committee. Captain Goggin testified: "I was emotionally stunned in going from household to household seeing children staring at walls with potentially tremendous energy but because they weren't getting food they were like zombies . . . I was stunned by the experience of driving in a White House limousine to an airport, going on a plane that was air-conditioned, in tremendous luxury, landing in Mississippi, Missouri, or California and going off in a car to a shack where children, in my opinion, were literally dying, their minds were dying.

"You come back to Washington and you try to explain this to somebody else, and you say, 'You must do something about it.' They say, 'Yes, we are going to do that, but for now we have tremendous budget problems and the Bureau of the Budget has great difficulties. We don't know where we are going to get the money.'

"I say, 'Yes, but people are dying out there.' Children are being condemned to totally wasted lives."

The two officers testified that in some rural counties welfare departments operated surplus food programs only when there was no farm work and that some county officials interpreted the rules so that those who were capable of work received no food.

The officers said the U.S. Department of Agriculture reports showing most of the counties in the nation had either food stamps or a surplus commodity program were misleading. Many of these programs existed only on paper. The officers said such paper programs did little to relieve the hunger of the undernourished poor.

Senator Allen Ellender asked Captain Goggin, "In most of the counties you visited, as I understand your report, you find that quite a few people who are entitled to food are not on the rolls, is that correct?"

Captain Goggin: "Yes, that is absolutely correct."

Senator Ellender asked why.

Captain Goggin: "Well, I think it is the local bureaucratic administrators of the programs and the local political officials in many cases."

In 1961 President John F. Kennedy issued an executive order: "The Secretary of Agriculture shall take immediate steps to make available for distribution, through appropriate state and local agencies, to all needy families a greater variety and quantity of food out of our agricultural abundance."

Congress created a food trust fund to put the policy to work; each year 30 percent of the customs duties are earmarked for the fund to finance distribution of commodities. The law allows the USDA to carry over $300 million from year to year. Any carryover above that amount must be turned over to the Treasury.

The emphasis was on "all needy families" and the instructions were clear. By this order, by laws and administrative regulations, the USDA was to help counties establish food programs for the needy. The USDA, however, is dominated by the southern plantation philosophies of rural Congressmen and Senators who control the agricultural purse strings. With them welfare is traditionally a local concern and the USDA could aid only those counties that asked for assistance.

As a result hundreds of rural counties had no programs to feed the hungry poor. Those counties that had requested commodity programs from the USDA—the USDA provides the food, the county pays the administration and distribution costs—often used the program to help farmers. Food was cut off when the harvest season started. A hungry family will work without questioning the pay.

Because so few counties were participating, the USDA was not utilizing all the money Congress had made available. Yearly through the 1960's the USDA turned $100 million to $225 million back to the Treasury.

By allowing the counties to refuse the programs, the USDA violated the law and shirked its administrative duties. Rural legal service attorneys across the nation filed a series of federal court actions to force the issue.

In Texas a federal judge ruled the USDA had to put federal

food programs in 109 counties within 60 days. The judge wrote: "Contrary to the intent of Congress . . . the [USDA] has determined that it will provide federal food assistance only in the counties where local government officials approve . . . ."

The California Rural Legal Assistance filed its first hunger suit in 1968, naming 21 of the state's 58 counties and the USDA as defendants. These counties had no food program. The class action was filed on behalf of hungry farm workers.

Federal Judge Stanley Weigel ruled: "The federal food programs at issue are intended to be, but are not now, benefiting the needy and the hungry persons in these counties. Unless the needy and hungry of these counties immediately receive the benefits of the federal food program for which they are the intended beneficiaries they will suffer immediate and irreparable harm, especially because there is limited work available during the winter months . . . ."

The judge agreed with the CRLA contention that the USDA had funds immediately available to feed the hungry and that the Secretary of Agriculture had full and unlimited authority to institute the commodity distribution programs in these counties. The judge ordered the hungry fed. The government appealed, but a three-judge panel upheld the decision. The hungry must be fed.

By this time most of the counties, acting on their own, began to comply, at least on paper, by applying for a federal food program. But a few still held out. Under the terms of Judge Weigel's order the USDA was required to institute a food program in each of the holdout counties at federal cost. The USDA, now under a new secretary, took no action.

CRLA attorneys went back into Judge Weigel's court and formally requested that the new Secretary of Agriculture Clifford Hardin be held in contempt. Before the judge could rule on the motion, the last of the counties voluntarily complied. The case was moot.

During the winter of 1968–69 rains and heavy fog reduced the already limited supply of winter work. Early in the spring of 1969 I drove through the San Joaquin Valley counties, trying to find out how farm workers' families were surviving these hungry months. Work had not opened up yet and few of the families had enough to eat.

In one primitive shantytown I asked a Black community worker where I could find hunger.

She replied: "Go knock on any door."

I did. She was right. Families had stretched their credit beyond the breaking point, some had managed to get on welfare, some were receiving surplus commodities once a month, but the supply issued was so meager not one family in ten said there was enough to last the month. Most were hungry.

Teachers working in poverty area schools could single out the hungry children by observing the symptoms. One child in five had hunger pains, headaches, was listless and uncomfortable. They had come to school without breakfast. They had no money for lunch.

Schools in some cities, like Fresno, routinely offered free lunches to the poor. The policy there was one of openness but a shortage of funds limited application of that policy. There was only enough money to meet one-third of the needs so a hungry child received a free meal every third day.

In smaller towns some of the districts offered "credit" and allowed the child to work off the "debt" by clearing tables or washing dishes. One school marked the credit tickets with the child's name and posted them on the bulletin board as a reminder that repayment was expected.

Credit was often limited. Once that limit was exceeded no lunch was available. In one school where credit was limited a teacher forced those children without funds and without credit to march into the cafeteria with the rest of the class. The hungry, moneyless children had to sit and watch others eat. When a newspaper reported the story, the school district's board of trustees cancelled the entire lunch program rather than comply with federal regulations. The farmer-taxpayers could not afford to administer a federally subsidized lunch program for the poor.

Nationally, the federal school lunch program costs over $400 million a year. It is administered by the USDA, in cooperation with local school districts. Hot lunches are available to all children for 35 to 50 cents. Those who cannot afford this subsidized price must be given a lunch free or at a further reduced price.

In a series of school lunch suits on behalf of farm worker children, CRLA contended 87 percent of these federal school lunch funds went to subsidize the hot lunches of the rich and middle-class children. CRLA charged that only one out of every ten needy children was receiving a free or reduced-price lunch as required by law.

After some legal sparring, the USDA settled out of court, conceding it did have the duty to insure that local school districts offered the poor free or reduced-cost lunches. CRLA then forced the USDA to comply with the law regulating the federal school milk program.

It is difficult to understand why the federal and local governments are so reluctant to feed the needy.

In 1970 the National Committee on Education of Migrant Children (NCEMC) reported: "The majority of migrant children we studied were hungry most mornings in school, did not receive a free lunch during the regular school year, did not receive even minimal health services . . . ."[8]

"That this callous neglect of basic human needs should exist concurrently with unspent migrant education budgets for food and health services is inexcusable." The NCEMC report revealed, "While migrant children went hungry, almost a million dollars [$954,986] or about 31 percent of the migrant education funds budgeted for food services, were not spent.

"Probably the most flagrantly indefensible denials of free lunch were encountered in Texas, where $578,000 or almost half of the 1969 Title I Migrant Amendment funds budgeted for food services were unspent and where migrant parents were subjected to humiliation and refusal when they requested free lunches which these funds were intended to supply."[9]

In Texas' Rio Grande Valley, there is widespread hunger and malnutrition. The Field Foundation sent 15 doctors into "El Valle" to study the problems of malnutrition and health care. Dr. Harry S. Lipscomb of the Baylor College of Medicine's Institute for Health Services Research said afterward, "I doubt that any group of physicians in the past 30 years has seen in this country as many malnourished children assembled in one place as we saw in Hidalgo County."

For a week the doctors worked out of Dr. Casso's clinic in McAllen. The team was supposed to study migrant family health, but the magnitude of the medical problems that confronted the doctors was overwhelming. They started almost immediately to treat diseases rather than study problems.

Dr. Lipscomb explained, "When you see human disease in a single individual you are concerned, whenever you see disasters you are involved deeply and overwhelmed, on a limited basis. But when you see a continuing stream, day after day, of large numbers of people who suffer the miseries of poor food, poor housing, poor clothing and what I consider inadequate health care, virtually no health care at all, there is a sort of a numbness that sets in after you see so many people . . . .

"Our team went down to see 50 families, and there were 900 people waiting in the street the day we got there. We were swamped. We worked day and night for five days. We went to study the families in depth, but the first child you saw with tape worms, hook worms, pin worms or with active ear infections or a pulmonary lesion, you were compelled—you had some visceral compulsion that made you have to treat these people. You couldn't turn them away.

"About two and a half hours after we started, every single doctor came in with this look of anguish. It was just overwhelming. They [families] all needed treatment, not just a checkup. We got on the phone to New York and called the Field Foundation. The Foundation agreed to pay for the drugs we had to order so I went across the street to the pharmacy.

"We inundated this poor fellow in twenty-four hours. He worked all night long. We were ordering iron, mineral, and vitamin preparations, antibiotics, superficial ointments for skin diseases, parasitisms, and fungus infections. By and large, it was primarily antibiotics for previously undetected, untreated infections and, of course, in the children, the untreated middle ear infections . . . . We found a significant number of children with really serious hearing loss from old, chronic, untreated, infected, draining ears. They had never had any care."

The loss of hearing to a child entering school presents a handicap. That handicap is compounded if the child's first language is Spanish and he or she has difficulty with English. Such chronic infections are persistent. The children usually have little or no concept of the progressive loss of hearing. When the child goes into a new class he is apt to head for the back of the room, to sit quietly. Neither he nor the teacher recognizes the hearing problem unless the child is tested.

The failure of federal, state, and local welfare programs to meet even the minimum nutritional needs; the lack of health care; the chronic, untreated medical problems they saw made Dr. Lipscomb and the others pessimistic. One of the Field Foundation team, Dr. Raymond M. Wheeler, told the Senate migrant labor subcommittee, "The children we saw that day have no future in our society. Malnutrition since birth has already impaired them physically, mentally, and emotionally. They do not have the capacity to engage in sustained physical or mental effort which is necessary to succeed in school, learn a trade, or assume the full responsibilities of citizenship in a complex society such as ours . . . ."

Dr. Wheeler, who has spent considerable time studying and treating the poor throughout the Southern states, said, "In our affluent money-oriented society, human needs of children have been subordinated to political and economic interests . . . . The farmer is not even prohibited from working young children in the fields if the parents, desperate for enough money to buy food and shelter, choose to take their children out of school or bring along their preschool-aged children to pick vegetables . . . ."

I asked Dr. Lipscomb about the effects of harvest work on children.

He said, "I can speculate. It is exceedingly difficult to prove. You know that in studies of stoop labor there are demonstrated X-ray changes in the vertebral bodies of stoop laborers . . . . If a child is anemic, has worms, is not eating adequately, has poor food mixture, especially if it is low in proteins, and some vitamins, if he cannot sleep adequately because of poor housing—couple all of this to physical labor and I would imagine it probably is not the sort of load he could carry very long. It might conceivably affect his ultimate longevity . . . ."

Dr. Wheeler told the senate subcommittee, "The migrant has a life expectancy 20 years less than the average American. His infant and maternal mortality is 125 percent higher than the national average. The death rate from influenza and pneumonia is 200 percent higher than the national rate . . . . We know from these statistics alone that migrant and seasonal farm workers live shorter lives, have more illnesses and accidents, lose more babies, and suffer more than the rest of us. Everything that we saw and heard in Florida and southwest Texas bore out this knowledge."

While in Florida and Texas Dr. Wheeler inspected public housing projects for farm workers and found "living conditions horrible and dehumanizing to the point of our disbelief. We saw living quarters constructed as long cinder block or wooden sheds, divided into single rooms by walls which do not reach the ceiling. Without heat, adequate light, or ventilation, and containing no plumbing, or refrigeration, each room no larger than 8 by 14 feet . . . the living space of an entire family, appropriately suggesting slave quarters of earlier days.''

Dr. Wheeler described the effect of living in such quarters: ''The absence of fresh air and the crowding greatly increases the likelihood of transmission of contagious diseases. This is why so many have tuberculosis as well as chronic respiratory infections.

''How is it possible for a child to study and perform in school when it is impossible for him to read by the light available to him? How can he possibly be emotionally well-adjusted when he has no privacy, when he lives in a cage? How can he possibly stay awake in school the following day when he has attempted to sleep in a bed with three or four of his brothers and sisters?''

The doctors who testified before Senator Mondale's committee, the doctors I have interviewed, and those writing in medical journals agree there is a serious lack of health care. Because of this even the most common seemingly unimportant irritants, like insect bites, can turn into major medical problems.

Dr. Gordon Harper was one of the Field Foundation medical team. He said, ''The first day we were working in Dr. Casso's clinic a young mother from Pharr brought in a baby, perhaps a year and a half old, complaining that his head and neck were swollen.''

The baby had a temperature of 106 degrees, his pulse was rapid and his respiration rapid; the child, though well developed and fairly well nourished, was acutely ill. The mother told Dr. Harper the boy had been bitten by insects two days before. An initially trivial infection turned into cellulitis, a bacterial infection of the skin and subcutaneous tissue. He treated the child and prescribed medication.

Later, testifying before Senator Mondale's subcommittee, Dr. Harper said, ''In Texas all of us saw windows without screening, open latrines, inadequate garbage disposal, standing water, and gaping holes in floors and walls. In Michigan I visited a migrant camp built literally right next to the municipal sewage pool and garbage dump. The stench was suffocating.

"Under these conditions insects and rodents thrive and attack the children playing or sleeping nearby. Once exposed to such bites, babies are much harder to keep clean and the bites more likely to be infected if homes have no running water.

"Not surprisingly, then, both in Texas and Michigan, infected bites are one of the most frequent conditions found in migrant children, directly related to the conditions they must live in. Superficial skin infections are common problems [and] treated promptly with good cleansing and a clean dressing and antibiotics as indicated, such an infection should never reach the proportions we found in McAllen."

Dr. Harper added, "But we learned how seldom poor people see doctors. A visit to a private doctor can cost $10 plus charges for medicine . . . . This mother, like so many, knew of no free dispensary. There was no outpatient or free emergency ward."

Dr. Casso explained there were no county hospitals to treat the indigent; there were proprietary or city-owned hospitals, but these were operated for profit or to at least pay for themselves. The poor were admitted to such hospitals only with great difficulty. Administrators often went to extraordinary lengths to collect from those impoverished patients they did admit.

Dr. Casso said, "There is no charity."

Throughout the 1960's the horrible picture of rural health care problems emerged from the hunger exposés by the media and from the U.S. Senate hearings on nutrition and migrant problems. Congress enacted a migrant health law and by 1970 appropriations were up to $14 million yearly for migrant health care; efforts were made to double the expenditure by 1972, but at best even the redoubled efforts were like applying Band Aids to a major wound and prescribing aspirin for the pain.

In Oregon 12 counties participate in the state's $500,000 migrant health program; 90 percent of the financing comes from the U.S. Public Health Service. The Oregon State Board of Health estimated 18,000 of the 40,000 migrant farm workers coming into Oregon each year had some contact with the program. Those seeking help are screened by state migrant health technicians and if a medical or dental problem is found the patient is referred either to a free clinic or to a private doctor or dentist. The private practitioners' bills are paid by the program.

California's Farm Worker Health Service was started on state funds in 1961. A decade later it was the oldest and one of the best migrant health projects in the nation. The program receives $1.4 million in federal funds and operates 33 clinics in 17 of the state's 42 major agricultural counties; in 1970 it served 24,000 seasonal farm workers and their families.

Such state reports can sound impressive—until they are compared with the total need. In Oregon less than half of the migrants were even seen, yet clinical reports show the farm workers there have the same kinds of medical problems as those reported by the Field Foundation doctors in the Rio Grande Valley.

The California Farm Worker Health Service officials report they only reach 15 percent of the state's seasonal farm workers. The problems of underfunding, a shortage of doctors and nurses, and a lack of physical facilities in which to conduct the clinics all contribute to this inability to cover more than a small portion of the need.

Most of these California clinics are operated as part of the state's migrant farm labor housing program. The state—financed by the federal government—built 26 seasonal farm labor housing centers. In addition to the housing, each of these centers has a day care center and preschool educational program, medical and dental clinics. Doctors and dentists from local communities donate their time to these clinics.

There are other federally assisted migrant clinics operated by schools and by county health departments, but in comparison to the need the number is limited. Most farm workers still receive little or no health care.

There are county hospitals for the indigent and many of these hospitals operate outpatient clinics. But conservative county governments have enforced regulations that intimidate the poor. In some counties farm workers who lived in the area and who were trying to establish their own homes had to sign a lien against any property they owned as they went into the hospital facilities. Those without property were screened for their ability to pay and were billed. Unpaid bills were turned over to bill collectors.

California has state Medi-cal and Medicare assistance programs operated through the county welfare departments, but Governor Ronald Reagan has been exercising much of his budget-cutting efforts here. Charity is not given easily, even in California.

Conservatism that orders civil servants to protect the tax dollar before they alleviate human need results in a waste of human life. When county politicians categorize welfare recipients as lazy individuals who would rather drink and lie around than work, their attitude directly influences the welfare services offered by that county.

When county politicians establish a policy of extracting some kind of payment for medical services offered the poor, the results begin to build a wall between that county's hospital and the indigent. Even if a county board of supervisors' intent was only to frighten away "deadbeats" and "chiselers" and to give "dignity" to those who could pay something of what they owed, the results were terrifying.

In Kern County, a very pregnant mother of seven brought the whole thing sharply into focus. She was a Mexican national, in California, by way of Texas, to work the harvest. She and her husband, with the help of the older children, had done fairly well the season before and they wanted to stay in

California. As we talked, through an interpreter, she was alone in a small, one-room labor camp cabin that had a lean-to kitchen tacked on the back. Her husband had the car and was out looking for work, the older children were at school, the younger ones were playing outside.

During the previous two weeks, her husband had earned $15. It had been like that all winter, a day or two of work a week, some weeks no work at all. Once, when they had absolutely nothing, they applied for welfare assistance. To do this they had had to. drive 20 miles in to the county seat. They had earned $200 the month before, and honestly reported this income. Their application was rejected.

The pregnant mother explained, "That lady [the welfare worker] told us we were lying, she told us we made more than that and she asked us, 'Why the hell you come to California? Why the hell don't you stay in Texas?'"

This husband and wife were in their late twenties, they had debts totaling $520. The money was owed to a loan company, a bank, a furniture store, an auto supply store, and the grocer who had allowed them enough credit to stay alive during the rainy winter.

Whether or not they were technically eligible for aid, the family was in obvious need. There were a few beans, some cereal, and a small bag of flour left in the kitchen. They had had no meat for weeks, there was no milk for the children. She had no telephone and no nearby friends to drive her to the county hospital, 20 miles away.

What would she do if the labor pains started?

She shrugged, "I would deliver the baby myself."

Had she done this before?

"Yes. Once. In Texas."

I got the impression she did not want to go to the county hospital, and I asked why.

"It would cost too much." She had heard, through friends, that she would have to pay $300, twice what she would have been charged in Texas. She said, "Of course, we don't even have enough to pay for such things in Texas either."

I asked the woman if she had attended any of the free prenatal clinics run by the county health department. She had, once. What had she learned?

"They gave me some pills, but I wasn't sick, so I threw them away."

She shrugged her shoulders again as she spoke. This shrug was not one of indifference, but of resignation. The medical services of the hospital were beyond her financial resources. The clinic was puzzling. She understood no English and the translation of the public health nurse's words made little sense to her. She understood medicine only in terms of crisis treatment.

As we talked, it was obvious this mother had accepted the inevitable. She had absolutely no control or influence over what was happening and what was about to happen. Both she and the child in her womb were undernourished, her diet for the past three months had been mostly corn tortillas, green chili, and beans.

She was worried about having enough milk to nurse the baby. She hoped her husband had found work so there would be enough food for her other children. These were things of immediate concern. Hospitals and clinics and doctors and preventative medicines and vitamins and eating specific nourishing foods—the nurse had passed out suggested diets in Spanish and English—were simply impractical thoughts. Such things were not possible.

Dr. Robert Coles, after his study of East Coast seasonal farm workers, said, "The migrant mother will work all during the pregnancy and travel is undertaken during the same period of time and finally the delivery is done in the rural cabin or in the fields.

"Fifty miles from Cape Kennedy one finds thousands of children who are receiving no medical care, who are living in the most abominable housing conditions and who are never even delivered in a hospital, never see a doctor, and whose infant mortality rate parallels the infant mortality rate of African and Asian nations . . . it is hard to accept the fact that in the second half of the twentieth century in the United States of America, women bear their children on the side of a road or in one-room houses which have rats and are without running water and electricity."[10]

The idea of a woman alone in a labor camp cabin delivering herself is frightening to me. I asked Dr. Casso if such a thing could be done successfully.

He explained, "Actually, if there is no complication, it is possible. But if she had a tear, or a hemorrhage, she would die."

Was it likely the baby would suffer some damage, say from lack of oxygen?

"It is possible because many of these babies are born depressed and you have to know how to stimulate them, make them breathe rapidly. For instance if after a baby is born it takes me 15 minutes to get him to breathe on his own and I don't give him oxygen and breathe for him, he will have some brain damage, maybe permanent damage because I didn't take care of him those first 10 or 15 minutes."

Dr. Casso has his own delivery room and small maternity ward in his office. Most of the expectant mothers come to him because they do not have enough money to pay the fees charged by the nearby McAllen hospital. He said the county's public health service did operate an obstetrics clinic but there were no arrangements to have the mothers delivered.

"They [the mothers] had to make such arrangements for themselves, so many of them were delivered in our clinic or by midwives. This [Rio Grande Valley] area is one of the places where midwives operate more actively than anywhere else in the nation." Dr. Casso said the infant mortality rate is higher in the Rio Grande Valley because of poor prenatal care, poor delivery care, poor nutrition on the part of the mother while she is carrying the baby, lack of medical facilities to take care of newborns.

He estimated 80 percent of the farm worker mothers are malnourished, and, as a result, the fetus is malnourished. "We see a lot of prematurity, a lot of prenatal complications as a result of poor nutrition. We get some bleeding, some abnormalities in the babies. All kinds of complications can happen because of poor nourishment.

"Now not all of them develop complications, but then there are also a lot of immeasurable factors, too. The baby can be born all right, be crying fine, but how much injury did the baby's brain suffer because of the mother's poor nutrition?"

This is perhaps the most disturbing question of all. The fetus is nurtured by the mother's blood and therefore one of the causes of fetal malnutrition is maternal undernutrition. Doctors know undernourishment affects the cellular structure of body organs.

Growth in any organ may proceed both by an increase in the number of cells, and an increase in the size of individual cells. Lack of protein inhibits cellular division, thereby limiting the number of cells within the organ to something less than normal. Malnutrition also restricts the growth of individual cells.

Dr. Myron Winick, professor of pediatrics at Cornell University, has written, "It would appear that the duration of malnutrition as well as the severity during this early critical period is extremely important in determining the ultimate cellular makeup of the brain."[11]

In humans the cell division progresses uniformly until birth, and then slows. By the end of the child's first year, there is very little cell division going on. Dr. Winick, an internationally recognized expert in this field, explained, "Malnutrition will curtail the rate of cell division in the brain if it is severe enough and if it occurs during the first year of life. If malnutrition continues into the second year of life not only is the number of cells reduced, but also the weight and protein per cell is reduced.''[12]

Dr. Winick said: ''During the past twenty years evidence has been mounting that an infant who has survived a period of severe malnutrition may be seriously handicapped—handicapped in terms of his physical and mental development. The implications of such evidence are staggering.

''The vicious cycle which is set in motion is self-perpetuating and continues from generation to generation. The malnourished infant growing up in poverty is unable to acquire the skills to deal with the complexities of modern society. The result is that he remains poor the rest of his life and his children are born into the same social and economic conditions.

''The family does not have the resources to adequately nourish the new infant. He in turn becomes seriously malnourished and, if able to survive, is handicapped in such a way as to prevent him from extricating himself from the plight of his parents. Thus the condition of poverty is perpetuated . . . .''[13]

Poverty recycles children into poverty. The parents pass on to the child a genetic potential at conception but by the time the infant is born that potential may have already been abridged by malnutrition.

8

> . . . many farm worker families consider it their right to take their own children with them . . . [into] . . . a shady orchard or vineyard, the fresh cool environment of a coastal lettuce field or a lush tomato field on a summer day. Some of these families consider it a basic freedom to allow their children to learn at an early age whatever values there are in earning a living . . . .
>
> *—Council of California Growers*

Power

The children are powerless. They are used by their parents, exploited by farmers, left unprotected by the government. Child labor laws are seldom enforced; those few cases brought before rural courts are heard by judges who quite often believe child labor on the farm is a valuable experience and a practice that should be encouraged.

As a result children of all ages can and do work at the third most dangerous occupation in the United States. They are part of a subservient labor force, a labor force that receives precious little reward for its sweat, a labor force that is without protection of the law, a labor force that is exploited because it is unorganized and powerless.

When new laws or amendments to existing laws are proposed to restrict the laissez-faire attitudes toward farm labor, grower organizations respond by passing resolutions and writing letters arguing that the exploitation of farm workers and their children must continue if the family farmer is to stay in business. Routinely groups like the National Council of Agricultural Employers and the American Farm Bureau Federation lobby against legislative efforts to extend labor laws to cover farm workers.

Farmers do not want workers to gain any toehold that would give them a chance to build a power base. This long-standing opposition to any change was summed up by the Washington State Agriculture Producers' Council in a 1967 letter to the governor. Here are some of the council's views:

"The agricultural industry is opposed to amendments [to labor laws] which would place farm employers in a position where they would be compelled to bargain with farm labor unions . . . .

"Inclusion of farm workers under the state unemployment compensation act seems difficult to administer . . . .

"As reliable farmers have adequate liability insurance to cover bona fide, on the job injuries, we do not believe it necessary to cover farm workers under the Washington State workman's compensation act . . . .

"We feel women and minors laws of Washington State should not be amended in a way to discourage children from farm work . . . ."

While farmers want no controls, they do favor the establishment of governmental services for workers in health, in education, in vocational training. The Washington farmers asked for federally funded child day care centers and they favored home economics instruction to teach migrant mothers how to get along on what the family earned. But they opposed removing the then current resident requirements for welfare assistance because "expanding welfare in such a form would make the state the haven for every welfare patron who found conditions unfavorable in his own state."

For those farm workers who remained through the winter to work on farms, the Washington farmers felt a welfare supplement to workers' incomes was justified because "winter farm wages which would equal public assistance income are not possible to pay, especially to a man with a large family."

Such public assistance to "underemployed" farm workers —available for several years in liberal welfare states like California—is a direct governmental subsidy to growers. Government-funded child-care centers, migrant education, and migrant health projects are also farm subsidies, because they are substitutes for worker income. These are Band Aids used to hold together a major wound. While each of these programs has direct benefits to the children and to the workers, they do nothing to alleviate the basic problem—low pay.

The problems faced by the farmer and the farm worker have their roots in economics and in the questions of power. The economics of farming are harsh realities that contradict romantic myths. Even so the romance of the westering pioneer is hard to dispel. The myth of the free enterprise system—of the rugged individual standing ready to risk his land and capital in the calculated gamble for profits—is even more difficult to put in perspective.

The free enterpise system—as it is verbalized by the Farm Bureau lobbies—sounds great. The American agri-business complex is without peer in its production capacities. The American farmer in 1972 could produce food and fiber for himself and 51 others—with the aid of billions of federal dollars and thousands of man days spent on research and development. The farmer has available to him a technological array of machines and chemicals that stagger the imagination. With the aid of the great agricultural universities and state colleges, the farmer has cut his labor needs and expanded his base of operation, making it possible for the American family to buy its food at very low prices.

The American farmer is the most efficient producer in the

world, if efficiency ignores the social costs, ignores the quality of the food produced, ignores the drastic changes imposed upon the life of the nation. What the voices of agriculture do not comment on is that by its very nature the free enterprise system allows only the fittest to survive. The ultimate result is predictable.

There were once thousands of family grocery stores; blacksmiths and cobblers and tinkers and coopers, all were once a part of the American social and economic fabric. All have disappeared, have been replaced by a supermarket society that substitutes quantity and glitter for quality and service. Why is the American farmer any different? The giant corporate-conglomerates are already moving in on the farm-to-supermarket food chain.

The competitive nature of the free enterprise system creates excesses that ultimately must be controlled by government if the society is to survive. From the very beginning child labor has been one of these excesses.

During the Industrial Revolution in England and in New England children were horribly exploited and the arguments that were used then to justify such exploitation are the same arguments being used today.

A 1910 report to the Congress noted: ''The traditions existing before the [1770's] revolution could not be changed suddenly or without knowledge of the new evils, a long way had to be gone over before child labor could be transformed from a righteous and beneficial into an unrighteous and socially harmful thing.''

During the previous century and a half the United States had been undergoing a transition from an agrarian to an urban-manufacturing society. But even in 1910 farming and the handcraft trades were traditionally the work of men. The newly created industrial jobs in the mills and factories were considered work for women and children. Thousands of children were employed for menial tasks, or as beasts of burden, and the justification was then—as now—that employment was the mother of virtue.

It was argued that idle children grow mischievous and delinquent. It was argued that by hiring women and children the industrialist was doing the public a service by keeping such people off the meager forms of public assistance then offered.

In the heavier industries that employed men, the excesses of management created intolerable conditions and these pressures in turn spawned industrial unions. The power of the workers forced changes. One of the longest battles was over child labor. It wasn't until the passage of the 1938 Fair Labor Standards Act that any effective laws were passed, and then the voice of agriculture was strong enough to block the inclusion of farm labor.

Today the tables are reversed; it is the organized industrial worker who performs ''man's work'' and farm labor is relegated to the powerless, to the men, women, and children who are so hungry, so poor, and so desperate they will work for the crumbs from agriculture's bountiful table.

A Presidential commission studied migrant labor in 1950 and found 395,000 children between the ages of 10 and 15 working on the farm. Twenty years later the U.S. Department of Labor reported 800,000 children less than 16 years old were working on the farms.

The commission reported to President Truman: ''The child labor to which we refer is not the chores and the vacation jobs children perform on their family's farm. The child labor of which we speak is that to be seen in large acreage of peas, snap beans, or cotton where children, sometimes as young as 5 and 6 years, work along with the adult members of the family at 'stoop labor.'

''Children work in agriculture because of the need to supplement their parents' earnings and because compulsory school attendance laws are not enforced. They also work, however, because their parents have no other place for them during their own work hours. A third factor is that some employers prefer children as workers.''

Two decades after those words were written the American Friends Service Committee reported, ''Children from the age of six work in the fields, harvesting the food we all eat. And children from infancy are too often just there, in the field, or sleeping in the cars not far away [like Jimmy Brooks]. The use of children as industrial laborers was outlawed under the Fair Labor Standards Act of 1938. Yet in 1970 one-fourth of the farm wage workers in the United States are under 16 years of age. Except for a change in locale—the work is done outdoors—the child labor scene in 1970 is reminiscent of the sweatshop scene of 1938 . . . children who work in agriculture are, for the most part, exempted from child labor laws and are practically abandoned to the discretion or whim of whoever's farm they are working on . . . .''

An exact comparison of the 1950 (395,000) and the 1970 (800,000) figures cannot be made because the age brackets do not match exactly. But these figures do indicate at least in a general way that child labor on the farm is increasing at a time when the total number of farm workers is declining. The USDA reports that between 1950 and 1970 the total number of farm workers declined from 4.3 million to 2.5 million. The biggest decline has come in the number of permanent jobs. Seasonal farm labor job statistics have remained relatively constant.[1]

As machines put men out of work they must seek alternate employment. Those who lose permanent jobs drop back into seasonal work. The Agribusiness Accountability Project—a Nader-type group—did a study on the effects of the federally subsidized agricultural college research programs on rural America: ''The turn to machinery has a snowball effect. As one crop is mechanized there is less work in the area; as two or three crops are mechanized, there is not enough work in the area to make a living, so the farm worker 'hits the road.'

Then there is a 'scarcity of labor' so other crops are mechanized.''[2]

When a machine puts heads of families out of work, when it makes them return to the migrant stream, the effect on the children is chaotic. Because the federal government spends nearly a half-billion dollars a year on research that helps the farmer mechanize, it would seem appropriate for the government to assume some responsibility for the displacement of workers. The USDA and the state land-grant colleges spend little time on the subject of impact on farm workers.

The Agribusiness Accountability report states: ''The land grant complex has been eager to work with the farm machinery manufacturers and with well-capitalized farming operations to mechanize all agriculture labor, but it has accepted no responsibility for the farm worker who is put out of work by the machine.''[3] In another section of the same report author James Hightower made this critical observation about the low cost of food to the consumer: ''In computing food prices, USDA does not add on the enormous social and cultural cost that also are products of the agricultural revolution. That cost is passed on first to the millions of humans who have been wasted by that revolution and secondly, to the consumer, whose higher taxes must help pay for those victims . . . .''[4]

Among these victims are the families who wander the face of the nation, searching for enough work to survive. In theory the U.S. Department of Labor is supposed to help these workers find jobs through the Rural Manpower Service, but here again the economic and political power is on the side of the grower, not the worker. RMS has come under attack by migrant legal aid lawyers who forced the Labor Department to critically examine this labor service. In 1972 a special Labor Department task force confirmed the service was grower-dominated and grower-oriented. This report stated: ''Without the economic and political power which comes from organization and solidarity, farm workers' interests suffered accordingly. They did not have the same protection under the minimum wage legislation as enjoyed by other workers, and their hourly wages consequently were normally lower. Their coverage under unemployment insurance, social security, and workman's compensation was nonexistent or restricted compared to coverage of nonagricultural workers.''

In other words farm workers were without power and this lack of power converts directly into economic privation for the worker and economic gain for the employer. Farmers in this nation save $3 billion a year by keeping farm workers subservient, by keeping them from obtaining the same power the industrial unions got after the 1935 Wagner Act established the National Labor Relations Board and the pro-union regulation of labor relations.

The 1972 Labor Department report of the RMS found ''farm workers are susceptible to exploitation by careless, insensitive, and even unscrupulous employers and social service workers. Yet individual workers generally are afraid to press their complaints because of the strength of the forces working against them—language barriers, fear of losing jobs, fear of eviction from bad, but scarce, housing, and other problems.''

The survey writers felt it would be a ''distinct advantage'' for farm workers to organize so that they would have an advocate to ''bring corrective pressure on any individual or institution who has treated [them] in violation of law or protection procedure. The role thus outlined is one traditionally performed by unions for their members.''

Without such an advocate, laws are not enforced; without such an advocate, the labor of children is exploited. The Labor Department reported: ''A state enforcement agent in California stated that he finds numerous minors in the fields during the summers who are under twelve or are working without permits. He feels that most violations concern out-of-state migrants and that it is more difficult for them to obtain work permits. He stated that he overlooks many of these summer violations because he feels there is no real harm in children working and that extensive enforcement would cause political ramifications because of the extensiveness of the problem.''

The report concluded: "Despite the large number of minors found to be illegally employed in agriculture each year by both federal and state enforcement officials, Department of Labor estimates indicate that officials only scratch the surface in terms of the total number of youth illegally employed. Few states set minimum age for children employed in agricultural work outside of school hours and those that do are sometimes lax about enforcement or are grossly understaffed.''

The enforcement of labor law has never been the traditional role of government without the application of power from some outside influence. Labor unions exert such power. This force acts as a counterbalance to the power exercised by the employer. Worker-controlled power is the ingredient essential to attaining such a balance.

Cesar Chavez, the charismatic farm labor organizer who successfully led California table-grape workers in the building of the United Farm Workers Union, has written: "It is necessary to build a power base. Money by itself does not get the job done. This is why poverty programs have such difficulty. Although many nice things are said and many wheels are spinning, very little real social change takes place. To change conditions without power is like trying to move a car without gasoline. If workers are going to do anything they need their own power.''

Chavez pointed out that while the workers have 1,000 votes on election day, they have been powerless; yet the grower, who has but one vote, can pick up the phone, call Washington, and be heard. Chavez concluded: "He [the grower] has more power because he has economic power. If we had economic power, our thousand votes would count a thousand times more than any individual's vote.''[5]

Antonio Orendain, the former illegal alien, the ''bracero'' contract worker, the ''green card'' legal alien who commuted across the border, then came to live and work in California and Texas, has the look of an Indian campesino; round face, almond eyes, a drooping mustache. He talks easily about his life as a mojado (wetback) and as a legal alien farm worker who finally became a citizen and a leader in the UFWU. His heavy, lyrical accent, his use of words, his syntax, make his speech poetic. The problems of farm labor trouble Orendain and he gives much thought to the underlying causes of these problems.

He says: "The American free enterprise system is a beautiful words—*the American Free Enterprise System.* If you have education, money, or a profession you can do a beautiful free enterprise system. But farm workers like me, we don't have education, we don't have any profession, we don't have any money, so my only free enterprise is if I am more hungry than you, I will have to work cheaper than you.

"Now what I am trying to say is the free enterprise system creates basic needs for everybody living in the system [but] you don't get enough money [as a farm worker] because you don't have enough education so they deny you the basic needs . . . .

"Any society is like when you get married, you create certain basic standards and certain basic needs. Kids have basic needs that you [as a father] meet. Maybe your kids have shoes and nice clean clothes, maybe mine have huaraches and nice clean clothes, we meet different basic needs.

"But say I have five kids and maybe three of them are real intelligent and have good grades in school, but the other two maybe they have real low grades, no? What happen if I tell the two guys with the low grades: 'Because you don't have the good grades, I not going to give you your basic needs. From now on I am not going to give you for huaraches, or I am not going to give you for pants unless you bring me the good grades from school.'

"This is exactly what society is doing against the farm worker.

We don't get enough money because they say we don't have enough education so they deny us the basic needs." Orendain feels the basic needs include the obvious food and shelter, but also the need for far more education than is available to workers and their families.

He says, "This is what I call discrimination more than just because you are black or white . . . this is discrimination on the basis of money, on basis of education, and basis of religion, and the religion forms a part of it, a part of the system, because for many centuries the priests teach you to be humble and to be nice and to be skinny and the more skinny you are, the more you suffer on earth, the easy way you can go through heaven."

Orendain continued, "They keep us poor and enslaving each other, they keep telling us that as soon as you get an education you can go higher and you can get your own slaves."

As he talked he gestured south, toward the Mexican border only a few miles away, where the poor stream across the international bridges seeking work on the farms. "They [farmers] tell us if we be nice, if we work hard and be good guys, we can be a boss or a contractor, but to do that I have to kiss ass, and I don't want to kiss nobody's ass."

Antonio Orendain wants to change the agri-business system, he knows the workers can make such a change only if they organize and use their collective power to determine their own destiny. He abhors governmental Band Aid programs because they keep workers dependent.

"Maybe they [the government] put up every fifty miles across the country a center where you get a doctor, a lawyer, and food and every goddamn thing you need for free because you are a poor guy. That way you have been castrated, automatically, as soon as you receive that thing you been castrated, because you can turn to the grower and say, 'You can pay me anything or don't pay me nothing,' or you don't have to go to work at all because everything is free."

Instead Orendain would have strong, independent men in

a strong union. "The union says, 'Give me an honest price for an honest day's work. Just give me enough for my basic needs.' If workers are given enough for the basic needs then they can decide for themselves what it is they want, and their children can learn to be lawyers or doctors or tractor drivers, whatever they want.

"Look, Lincoln did not become a lawyer because of the federal government. He became a lawyer because he created the idea first, and when you give me [enough pay] for my basic needs, when I have enough food in my stomach, then I start thinking I want to be a lawyer, want to be a doctor, and I create the idea and I am willing to sacrifice everything for my idea."

Orendain was objecting to the governmental retraining programs that shift the farm worker from one job to another, that train field labor to drive tractor or to weld or go into mechanical repair work. "As you move field workers into another skill, you create a vacuum, it must be filled by another worker. The low-paying job still exists. The farm worker may make 95 cents moving earth with a tool [shovel] that a union construction worker makes $3 an hour for. The question is not to move the guy [farm worker] from here to there [a construction job] but to raise the wages on the farm."

Union men like Orendain are obviously advocates of a cause, they are locked in a national battle with the farm employers. The issues the union raises, the defenses raised by the growers, generate great controversies. As these controversies develop it is too easy to fall into the emotional trap of choosing up sides and arguing "good guys" versus "bad guys." But such argument avoids the basic issues. The contest between worker and employer is essentially an economic power struggle.

To date, the farmer's economic and political power have prevailed. Farmers have always had a cheap supply of labor and have been able to exploit that labor because the general society has sanctioned such exploitation in the name of the family farm and a cheap supply of food. (The USDA brags that the American consumer spends only 16 percent of his disposable income for food because of the economic efficiency of agri-business.)

While the plight of the family farm is publicized, while billions of dollars are spent propping up what is called the family farm economy, there are great profits being made in agri-business. Profits are earned by great corporations that grow, process, and market farm products as one part of a complex of corporate interests. Profits are generated by those who enter into tax-loss farming that allows nonagricultural corporations and individuals to write off land improvements while converting high income tax bracket money into capital gains ventures.

But these kinds of profits are generally hidden from public view. The public sees and hears the poor farmer fighting to keep his costs down, trying to prevent farm workers from gaining enough power to force labor costs higher. Some try to gain public support for the farmer by arguing an increase in wages would force the cost of food up. Such argument obscures the fact that only a small portion of the consumer's dollar goes into farm labor costs; most of the cost of food is in the processing and marketing. For instance, a head of lettuce costing 21 cents has one or two cents' worth of field labor built in. If wages were doubled it would cost but a few pennies more.

However, the doubling of the wage has serious effect on the small farmer who is tottering on the brink of bankruptcy. Farm labor costs make up one of the biggest single cash outlays in the operation of a fruit or vegetable farm. It is not uncommon for a small San Joaquin Valley fruit grower to pay out $50,000 to $75,000 in wages.

As wages have gone up—union activities in California over the past decade have almost doubled the wage scale, raising it from $1.10 an hour in 1960 to $2 an hour in 1970—the traditional answer has been for farmers to mechanize. The USDA and the agriculture colleges develop the machines, private industry builds them, and those farmers that can afford the $15,000 to $30,000 cost per machine, replace their hand labor crews.

The question of mechanization has become one of the most critical facing union efforts among farm workers. The UFWU, in its wine vineyard contracts in California, has had to take a "no machines" position because the industry refused to accept responsibility for workers displaced by mechanization. Thus far the UFWU has renegotiated three contracts with large vintners with provisions that exclude harvest machinery.

UFWU chief counsel Jerome Cohen said, "This was a very big issue. We are still willing to negotiate if they [the wine industry] are willing to talk about retraining and relocating workers that are displaced by machines."

Cohen said the giant Heublein Corporation had tentatively agreed not to use wine-grape harvesting machines in its established vineyards if the UFWU would agree to allow machine harvest of new plantings. The UFWU agreed, if a percentage of the profits from the mechanically harvested crop would be used to aid workers who would normally have had such work. The agreement was contingent upon the entire wine industry's approving the idea. Heublein could not get such an accord and the UFWU dropped back to a total "no machine" position.

The costs of such retraining could be worked into a farm-to-market pricing package and the companies would still show a profit. Mechanization—to the large corporate farm—is no different than mechanization in other industries. When the International Longshoremen and Warehousemen's Union agreed to allow containerization on the docks in exchange for $30 million a year from the Pacific Maritime Association's member companies the idea sounded radical. The funds were to be used for early retirement for those workers replaced. The $30-million-a-year cost was only a small percentage of the total *new* profits made by these companies.

Writing about the ILWU or about mechanization and USDA-funded research may sound like a drift away from the subject of child labor, but it is not. Children work on farms because their parents are powerless to force employers to pay more, powerless to do anything about being displaced by federally developed machines. To date the federal, state, and county governments have not faced the responsibilities of their actions in this sphere. As a matter of public policy they have solved mechanical-technological problems that benefit the larger, successful growers at the expense of both the small farmer who cannot afford such machines and the worker.

Over the years the advancement of farm technology has been the USDA's prime function. It has assumed the ostrich position on such side issues as the displacement of already poverty-ridden farm workers, hoping that by ignoring the "migrant problem" it would disappear.

Great bureaus of government, while they bend with the political winds, are all but impervious to outside influence that would bring about any real change. Even in the most liberal administrations the intent of the President and his advisors is often frustrated by this impregnability. The bureaucrat, protected and guided by the self-interest of a few powerful legislators, is nonresponsive to change.

When President John F. Kennedy ordered the hungry fed, he was no more successful than Henry Wallace had been thirty years earlier when—as Secretary of Agriculture—he ordered all the hungry fed.

Orville Freeman wrote in 1968: "The anomaly of hunger in the midst of abundance is what led me to accept President Kennedy's invitation to become Secretary of Agriculture in the first place. I have been trying to do something about it ever since."

At the time Freeman was on the defensive, responding to a CBS-TV documentary that both exposed the hunger in the nation and pointed to the shortcomings of the USDA's food programs.

Two years later Washington columnist TRB wrote about taxes

and hunger and Sunflower County, Mississippi. In the column
he quoted an exchange between an investigator and a mother:
"No fresh milk?"
"No, sir."
"Do they get milk, the small ones?"
"No. Ain't no one of them has milk every day. They lucky
to get it twice a month. Sometimes they cry."

Then TRB observed: "Lots of unemployment in Sunflower
County. You see, the government, with my taxes, pays cotton
producers not to grow cotton. Naturally that puts farm hands
out of work. It's a funny thing. There were 6 million farms
in 1940 and 3 million today and yet the number of county
agents has increased (6,800 to 10,200). The Agriculture Department had a staff of 84,000 to service 20 million people on
farms 20 years ago; now there are half as many farms but
the Department rolls have grown to 125,000."

The bureaucracy grows, but is nonresponsive to the needs
of the hungry. TRB explained that among the farms receiving
$3.5 billion in federal crop subsidies that year was a $146,792
payment to Eastland Plantations, Inc. TRB wrote: "Yes, siree,
that's Jim Eastland, our Jim, who's chairman of the Senate
Judiciary Committee and a member of the Agriculture Committee."

Senator Eastland is just one of a handful of legislators who
favor the Southern plantation form of agricultural enterprise
and who hold key positions on the committees that control
the purse strings. Their power, in concert with the bureaucrats,
is unbeatable.

On the issues of welfare, of farm labor, of child labor on
the farm they have decreed the USDA will follow a policy
of local control; local governments are allowed to administer
the federal programs, and local governments are controlled by
agri-business interests in farming areas. The workers, without
power, are helpless.

The emergence of the United Farm Workers Union during

the past decade has caused the agri-business–Southern plantation power structure to shift positions a bit. After keeping farm labor outside the National Labor Relations Act for 35 years, farm block politicians—at the behest of organizations like the American Farm Bureau—are proposing new laws to allow farm workers the right to organize, but only under conditions established by the agriculture industry.

In Idaho, Kansas, and Arizona, state legislatures have passed "labor" bills that allow a limited number of farm workers to vote by secret ballot to form a union, but which prevent the newly formed union from using any of the economic weapons that would put such a union on equal footing with the growers. The laws prevent effective strikes and outlaw the secondary boycott. The same kind of legislation has been proposed in all the farm states and at the federal level. Such legislation—if it is found to be constitutional—would effectively disarm the UFWU and leave the workers powerless.

In 1972 the Los Angeles *Times* ran an opinion piece I wrote exposing the use of child labor on the farm and then a few weeks later used much of the information I had developed in an editorial that was critical of farm labor practices. In response to this editorial, O. W. Fillerup, Executive Vice-President of the Council of California Growers, wrote:

"Your editorial [April 30] about farm labor and child labor in California and elsewhere paints with a very broad brush, thereby obscuring much of the detail necessary to understanding and remedying these matters. The language tends to inflame the issue emotionally, which is a mistake.

"It is also a mistake to try to link the employment of children specifically with the farm labor issue . . . child labor on farms in California . . . does not occur because of oppression by agricultural employers, and is not always the result of the family's economic need.

"Agricultural employers receive little if any benefit when minors spend time in their fields. While your editorial made it appear that employers expect work from children, they don't even encourage it . . . overstating the case for farm workers and children and charging scandals where none exist do not encourage reasoned and helpful solutions.''

It was Fillerup's contention that ''if we are to have more than superficial understanding of this matter, we must know those who make up the farm labor force. Nobody is closer to these people in California than agricultural employers. Any worthwhile solution to the matter of farm labor, including the presence of minors on farms, must include the counsel of agricultural employers—farmers and growers—who have established unusually close relationships with their workers through the years.''

Obviously any solution must involve both the farmer and the farm worker, but such involvement must be based on the strengths of each, not on the farmer's paternalism. As it stands now the farmer and the farm worker are struggling for a greater piece of the same dollar. Children are a pawn in this struggle. At present the worker needs the hands of his wife and his children just to hang onto enough of that dollar to survive. If the worker is to receive a larger share of that dollar he must take it by economic force.

Child labor may not be a significant factor in farming, if the measure is the volume of their production. A 10-year-old boy does not pick as many tomatoes or grapes as his 30-year-old father. But the fact that he is there, in the vines, assisting the family means the family is less likely to go hungry; the child picks and what he earns goes for clothing or food or rent.

Ironically, farmers give proof of the importance of the children's working by arguing that if child labor laws are enforced the families will leave and go where children can work. This was the reason given in Louisiana for creating a special migrant school that allowed the children to put in a full morning picking strawberries before they started classes. When the National Committee on the Education of Migrant Children brought in the U.S. Labor Department to force the discontinuance of this practice in the spring of 1972, the action did not disrupt the strawberry harvest as predicted.

NCEMC Director Casandra Stockburger said, "No farmer reported losing any of his crop because of the absence of children."

Where the child labor issue has been forced farmers have found they can do without the labor of children. Farm workers will leave their children behind if a general crackdown on child labor is enforced. But the enforcement of existing laws and the application of the Band Aid migrant programs are only temporary solutions at best.

There must be drastic change in the basic agri-business system itself. The small farmer is caught between the worker unrest and the corporate-conglomerate giants that are taking over great chunks of agricultural production. These huge corporations are vertically integrated—they do everything from plant the seed to wrap the product and sell it to the housewife—and their influence on markets, wages, and working conditions sets the pattern. Often the small farmer finances his year-to-year farming costs through one of these giants and then, at year's end, he must sell his crop through the giant's marketing operations. The big corporation makes a profit on the financing and on the marketing. The small farmer's chances of paying off his debts, commissions, and fees and still making a profit are growing slimmer.

In October of 1960, Fred Van Dyke, a San Joaquin Valley farmer who favored the unionization of farm labor, gave a talk to a church group in Stockton. He said: "I don't care what argument the Associated Farmers and Farm Bureau may advance. They complain about a cost-price squeeze. They claim that agriculture is unique because it deals with perishable commodities. They complain about the unpredictability of the weather. All this is so much sophistry, rationalization, and evasion.

"All of it is irrelevant when compared to one single child weeping from hunger . . . . The moral argument, the humanitarian argument, closes debate without any further evidence required. The argument based upon conscience demands —and I say demands—that existing arrangements in agricultural labor be rethought and rebuilt from the very ground up. The question of how this is to be done is secondary. The first step is to recognize that it must be done . . . ."

Van Dyke's outspoken position, at a time when the AFL-CIO was actively organizing farm labor in the San Joaquin Valley, earned the wrath of his fellow farmers. He had hoped the strength of his logic would sway his neighbors, but then he came to believe, "There is only one force in our society of countervailing forces which can bring about this change: the force of organized labor."

In his speech, he concluded: "You say to me, 'That will mean giving up freedom and independence.' I say to you that the only freedom the average farmer has today is the freedom to go broke. And I say to you that bankruptcy is the shortest road to slavery. The day that men representing me and my fellow farmers sit down across the table from men representing the laborers who work for us, will in fact be an Independence Day for farmers . . . we will be free from our own excesses under a system . . . which has been marked not by freedom, but by license."

Van Dyke's words were rejected. He was scorned. During the following decade the demise of the small farmer was accelerated in direct relation to the increased influence of the corporations and conglomerates entering farming. The giants' control became more firmly fixed.

Eleanor Eaton, Rural Affairs Director of the American Friends Service Committee, testifying before the House Agricultural Labor Subcommittee in 1971, said, "The small farmer is squeezed by corporate giants and as a result says that he would go out of business if he had to pay the same minimum wage as do the industries to whom he sells his products. In New Jersey the Migrant Ministry reports that Campbell's had paid farmers the same price for tomatoes, $42.08 per ton, for the past four years. In Oregon in 1970 workers received 3 cents a pound for picking pole beans, the same rate they received for the last four years . . . .

"The small farmer is in a vulnerable position. Too often he is made the villain when he is not. But he has options; he has alternatives, as the midwest farmers who have formed the National Farmers Organization have realized. The farm worker has no alternatives, no options; he must either accept what is offered or go totally hungry, and he must utilize the hands and bodies of his children to increase the number of pounds picked by his family.

"The myth still persists that working in agriculture is good for children; that it teaches them value of money; that when we talk about children in agriculture we are talking about work in fresh unpolluted open air in the cool mornings; that children learn they have duties as well as privileges; that they learn the value of hard work and of a dollar.

"This may be true for kids who have privileges; who work when and as long as they want to; who keep what they earn and can buy a bicycle or extra clothes; who had a good start in life with proper medical care; who go home at night to a good bed, a good meal, and start work after a good breakfast.

"But how does the migrant child learn the value of work when he sees his parents and brothers and sisters work long hours, six days a week—or sit around the fields waiting for work—and still there are only beans for supper . . . .

"The problem of child labor in agriculture is inseparable from the problems of the farm workers and in a larger sense from the responsible corporate policy and improved agricultural management and labor management relations. Farm workers will need to take their kids out of school, to put them to work in the fields, until they get the same wages, protections, and rights as industrial workers."

The AFSC recommended farm workers be covered by an adequate minimum wage of $2.25 an hour and recognized that to achieve this the federal government "may have to subsidize the farm worker as we now do the airlines, the aerospace industry, the corporate giants, the growers, and the farmers." The AFSC would have farm labor returned to the 1935 Wagner Act, unamended, to give them the tools to build a strong union; it would eliminate child labor on the farm; it would have Congress appropriate enough money to implement the enforcement of existing regulatory laws; it would extend unemployment insurance and increase day care centers.

The key to the solution is found in the midst of these recommendations. If farm workers are granted the same rights to organize as the industrial workers had in the last half of the 1930's, they can and will build a strong union. Without a strong advocate little will change. The simple passage of new laws, the development of Band Aid programs—no matter how well conceived and executed—will not solve the basic problems.

Children should not *have* to work. They should not be *used* to depress the labor market, should not be used to take the place of breadwinners. I think it time the farmer comes out from behind the mythology and admits that the need for child labor is rooted in economics. Farm workers do not make enough to support their families and until they do their children must work.

It is true that the child labor problem is intricately tied into the larger complexities of farm economics. If the family farm is salvageable—and there is doubt that salvage is possible even with drastic changes—some kind of controls are going to have to be imposed on corporate and conglomerate farmers who ma-

nipulate great profits and tax advantages out of the rural countryside.

If the unionization of farm labor runs its course without
workers, farmers, and the government recognizing and dealing
with these other problems of farm economics, the small farmer
will be speeded into oblivion. As a result control of agriculture
will shift into the hands of conglomerates like General Motors
and ITT. Then farm workers will be unionized, child labor
will be eliminated, but the family farm will no longer exist
and the quality of food will be immeasurably reduced.

The family farm will go the way of the mom and pop grocery store, of the village blacksmith shop and the cobbler's
bench. The process is already far advanced. The quality of
food has already deteriorated, with fruits and vegetables "en-
gineered" by land-grant colleges to withstand machine harvest
and to look pretty; if this trend is to be stopped, the small
farmers must collectively gather their strengths and force
buyers to give them a fair return for their product. The
government should aid them in this effort, just as it should
aid the farm worker in collectively gathering his
strength for a contest with the grower.

But this government aid should not include handouts. Congress can and should legislatively clear the way for both farmer
and farm worker to make a concerted effort on their own behalf.
The government should inhibit unbridled expansion of tax-
write-off farming and the conglomerate manipulation of the
national food source and supply systems. It might be that a
federally structured commission—similar to the Public Utilities
Commission—could be designed to regulate the public interest
in the source and supply of food. Food is too basic a necessity
to be left to the unfettered avarice of free enterprise. Such
a commission could guarantee fair collective bargaining and
favorable profit margins by exercising control over the excess
profiteering at any level, and fixing a consumer price that did

not provide the American table a low-cost meal at the expense of a child's future.

Child labor on the farm must be stopped. The cost in human lives is too great, the waste of human potential too much to throw away. The life of a Jimmy Brooks or a Michael Hays is too high a price to pay for farm profits. The recycled poverty of the children of the Black, the Brown, the Anglo farm worker is too great a pain to suffer; the heartless bureaucratic responses to hunger and need too great a stain on the national honor to be tolerated.

The myths must be put to rest once and for all. The farm is not a good place for children to work, just as no factory, no mine, no cotton mill is a good place for children to work. To argue that the farm is different, to call the fields lush and cool and the air unpolluted, is a callous effort to mask the truths of child labor. It is time we put such nonsense aside, it is time that we all—the urban and the rural communities—begin to seek solutions that will guarantee these children a healthy, productive future.

Notes

Chapter 1   The Myths

1. This quote comes from the reprint of a debate between Senator Thomas and Owen R. Lovejoy, general secretary, National Child Labor Committee, New York City. The debates were reprinted in publication 326 of the National Conference of Social Work for the National Child Labor Committee, June 12, 1925.

2. *Child Labor in Agriculture, Summer 1970*, American Friends Service Committee, Philadelphia, 1971, p. 1.

3. Salem (Ore.) *Capitol Journal*, March 24, 1971.

4. This figure is an estimate based on a combination of U.S. Department of Labor and U.S. Department of Agriculture statistics that establish the rates of pay for farm workers and for industrial workers and the number of man days of labor used in agriculture. If farmers paid industrial wages for the 201,000,000 man days of labor estimated by the USDA it would cost them an additional $3 billion.

5. *Working Children: A Report on Child Labor*, U.S. Department of Labor, WH Publication 1323, April 1971, p. 7.

6. *Annual Rural Manpower Report, 1970*, Oregon State Employment Service, Salem, 1970.

7. *Child Labor in Agriculture, Summer 1970*, American Friends Service Committee, Philadelphia, 1971, P. 43.

8. *New York Times*, April 26, 1971.

9. *Domestic Migratory Farm Workers*, Agriculture Economic Report 121, U.S. Department of Agriculture, September 1967.

10. *The Hired Farm Working Force of 1970*, Agriculture Economic Report 201, U.S. Department of Agriculture.

11. Such accidents are reported in brief anecdotes for each year in *Working Children, A Report on Child Labor*, U.S. Department of Labor Publication WH 1323.

Chapter 2   Jimmy's Dead

1. *Migrant and Seasonal Farm Worker Powerlessness*, Hearings Before the U.S. Senate Subcommittee on Migratory Labor, August 1, 1969, Vol. 6–A, p. 3217.

2. *Migrant and Seasonal Farm Worker Powerlessness*, Hearings Before the U.S. Senate Subcommittee on Migratory Labor, August 7, 1969, Vol. 4-A, pp. 1253–54.

3. *Ibid.*, p. 1250.

Chapter 3   On the Season

1. Dr. Robert Coles testified before the U.S. Senate Subcommittee on Migratory Labor on July 28, 1969 (*Migrant and Seasonal Farm Worker Powerlessness*, Vol. 2, pp. 334–459). In addition to his extensive testimony, Dr. Coles made available to the committee a working draft of "Uprooted Children," a portion of the second volume of *Children of Crisis*. Much of Dr. Coles' testimony before the committee is repeated in his written work. Dr. Coles' extensive work with migrant children presents a unique and valuable contribution to understanding their tragic existence.

2. *Migrant and Seasonal Farm Worker Powerlessness*, Hearings Before the U.S. Senate Subcommittee on Migratory Labor, July 16–17, 1969, Vol. 3-B, pp. 1094–9.

3. *Earnings of Migratory Farm Workers in Wayne County, New York: 1968*, J. Bryce Herrington, Monograph #1, State University College, Genesco, New York.

4. *Migrant and Seasonal Farm Worker Powerlessness*, Hearings Before the U.S. Senate Subcommittee on Migratory Labor, July 28, 1969, Dr. Coles' testimony, Vol. 2, pp. 338–41.

Chapter 4   Los Trabajadores

1. *Staff Report, Farm Workers*, U.S. Commission on Civil Rights, 1969.

2. David North, *The Border Crossers*, A Study for the U.S. Department of Labor by the Trans-Century Corporation, April 1970, p. 13.

3. *Ibid.*, p. 5.

4. *Ibid.*, Prologue, pp. v–vi.

5. *Migratory Labor in Ohio*, Report of the Governor's Committee, August 1968, p. 53.

6. *Migrant and Seasonal Farm Worker Powerlessness*, Hearings Before the U.S. Senate Subcommittee on Migratory Labor, April 14, 1970, Vol. 7-A, pp. 4051–2.

7. *Migrant and Seasonal Farm Worker Powerlessness*, Hearings Before the U.S. Senate Subcommittee on Migratory Labor, August 7, 1969, Vol. 4-A, pp. 1349–1415.

Chapter 5   Law Enforcement

1. *Annual Rural Manpower Report, 1970*, Oregon State Employment Service, Salem, 1970, p. 28.

Chapter 6   Lección, Escritura y Aritmética

1. David Ballesteros, "Toward an Advantaged Society: Bilingual Education in the 70's," *The National Elementary Principal*, Vol. 50, no. 2, November 1970, p. 25.

2. Vidal A. Rivera, "The Forgotten Ones: Children of Migrants," *The National Elementary Principal*, Vol. 50, no. 2, November 1970, p.41.

3. *Wednesday's Children*, National Committee on the Education of Migrant Children, New York, 1971, p. iii.

4. *Ibid.*, p. 24.

5. *Ibid.*

6. *Ibid.*, p. 74.

7. *Ibid.*, p. 75.

8. *Migrant and Seasonal Farm Worker Powerlessness*, Hearings Before the U.S. Senate Subcommittee on Migratory Labor, July 28, 1969, Vol. 2, pp. 350–51.

Chapter 7   Hunger: Knock on Any Door

1. Dr. Chase has reported the results of this study to Senator George McGovern's Select Committee on Nutrition and Human Needs and has written it up in "Nutritional Status of Preschool Mexican-American Migrant Farm Children," in the *American Journal of Diseases of Children*, Vol. 122, October 1971, p. 316.

2. *Migrant and Seasonal Farm Worker Powerlessness*, Hearings Before the U. S. Senate Subcommittee on Migratory Labor, July 20, 1970, Vol. 8-A, p. 5123.

3. *Nutrition and Human Needs*, Hearings Before the U.S. Senate Select Committee on Nutrition and Human Needs, February 18, 1969, Vol. 4, pp. 1162–3.

4. *Ibid.*, p. 1197.

5. *Ibid.*, p. 1212.

6. *Ibid.*, p. 1214.

7. *Ibid.*, pp. 1203–4.

8. *Wednesday's Children*, National Committee on the Education of Migrant Children, New York, 1971, p. 77.

9. *Ibid.*, p. 81.

10. *Migrant and Seasonal Farm Worker Powerlessness*, Hearings Before the U.S. Senate Subcommittee on Migratory Labor, July 28, 1969, Vol. 2, p. 337.

11. Myron Winick, M.D., "Fetal Malnutrition," *Clinical Obstetrics and Gynecology*, Vol. 13, no. 3, September 1970, p. 535.

12. *Ibid.*, p. 537.

13. Myron Winick, M.D., "Nutrition and Mental Development," *Medical Clinics of North America*, Vol. 54, no. 6, November 1970, p. 1413.

Chapter 8   Power

1. *The Hired Farm Working Force of 1970*, Agriculture Economic Report 201, U.S. Department of Agriculture, 1971.

2. Jim Hightower, *Hard Tomatoes, Hard Times*, Agribusiness Accountability Project, Washington, 1972, p. 53.

3. *Ibid.*, p. 8

4. *Ibid.*, p. 35.

5. Mark Day, *Forty Acres*, New York, Praeger, 1971, pp. 9–11.

Bibliography

Books

Berger, Samuel R., *Dollar Harvest: The Story of the Farm Bureau* (Lexington, Mass.: D. C. Heath and Company, 1971).

Bishop, C. E., ed., *Farm Labor in the United States* (New York: Columbia University Press, 1967).

Coles, Robert, *Children of Crisis: Migrants, Sharecroppers, Mountaineers*, Volume II (Boston: Little, Brown and Company, 1971).

Day, Mark, *Forty Acres: Cesar Chavez and the Farm Workers* (New York: Praeger Publishers, 1971).

Dunne, John Gregory, *Delano: Revised and Updated* (New York: Farrar, Straus and Giroux, 1971).

Friedland, William H., and Dorothy Nelkin, *Migrant: Agricultural Workers in America's Northeast* (New York: Holt, Rinehart and Winston, 1971).

Galarza, Ernesto, *Spiders in the House and Workers in the Field* (Notre Dame, Ind.: University of Notre Dame Press, 1970).

Grebler, Leo, Joan W. Moore, and Ralph C. Guzman, *The Mexican-American People: The Nation's Second Largest Minority* (New York: The Free Press, 1970).

Hunger, U.S.A.: A Report by the Citizens' Board of Inquiry into Hunger and Malnutrition in the United States (Boston: Beacon Press, 1968).

London, Joan, and Henry Anderson, *So Shall Ye Reap* (New York: Thomas Y. Crowell Company, 1970).

Matthiessen, Peter, *Sal Si Puedes: Cesar Chavez and the New American Revolution* (New York: Random House, 1969).

McWilliams, Carey, *Factories in the Field: The Story of Migratory Farm Labor in California* (Santa Barbara: Peregrine Publishers, Inc., 1971).

Samora, Julian, *Los Mojados: The Wetback Story* (Notre Dame, Ind.: University of Notre Dame Press, 1971).

Wright, Dale, *They Harvest Despair: The Migrant Farm Worker* (Boston: Beacon Press, 1965).

Wednesday's Children: A Report on Programs Funded Under the Migrant Amendment to Title I of the Elementary and Secondary Education Act (New York: National Committee on Education of Migrant Children, 1971).

U.S. Government Documents and Reports

U.S. Congress. House. Committee on Education and Labor. *Employment of "Green Card" Aliens During Labor Disputes, Hearings* before the Special Subcommittee on Labor of the Committee on Education and Labor (Washington, D.C.: Government Printing Office, 1969).

U.S. Congress. House. Committee on Education and Labor. *Seminar on Farm Labor Problems, Hearings* before the Subcommittee on Agricultural Labor of the Committee on Education and Labor (Washington, D.C.: Government Printing Office, 1971).

U.S. Congress. House. Select Committee on Nutrition and Human Needs, *The Food Gap: Poverty and Malnutrition in the United States* (Washington, D.C.: Government Printing Office, 1969).

U.S. Congress. Senate. Committee on Labor and Public Welfare. *Migrant and Seasonal Farmworker Powerlessness, Hearings* before the Subcommittee on Migratory Labor of the Committee on Labor and Public Welfare, 16 volumes (Washington, D.C.: Government Printing Office, 1970).

U.S. Congress. Senate. Select Committee on Nutrition and Human Needs. *Nutrition and Human Needs, Hearings* before the Select Committee on Nutrition and Human Needs, Part 4 (South Carolina) and 5A (Florida) (Washington, D.C.: Government Printing Office, 1969).

U.S. Congress. Senate. Select Committee on Nutrition and Human Needs. *Nutrition and Human Needs, Hearings* before the Select Committee on Nutrition and Human Needs, Part 3 (Washington, D.C.: Government Printing Office, 1970).

U.S. Congress. Senate. Select Committee on Nutrition and Human Needs. *Poverty, Malnutrition, and Federal Food Assistance Programs: A*

Statistical Summary (Washington, D.C.: Government Printing Office, 1969).

U.S. Congress. Senate. *Woman and Child Wage-Earners in the United States: Volume VI—The Beginnings of Child Labor Legislation in Certain States, a Comparative Study*, by Elizabeth Lewis Otley, Senate Document 645, 61st Congress, 2nd Session (Washington, D.C.: Government Printing Office, 1910).

U.S. Congress. Senate. *Woman and Child Wage-Earners in the United States: Volume VII—Conditions Under Which Children Leave School to Go to Work*, by Charles P. Niell, Senate Document 645, 61st Congress, 2nd Session (Washington, D.C.: Government Printing Office, 1910).

U.S. Department of Agriculture. Economic Research Service. *Domestic Migratory Farmworkers: Personal and Economic Characteristics*, USDA Agricultural Economic Report No. 121, Washington, D.C., September 1967.

U.S. Department of Agriculture. Economic Research Service. *The Hired Farm Working Force of 1970: A Statistical Report*, USDA Agricultural Economic Report No. 201, Washington, D.C., 1971.

U.S. Department of Agriculture. Office of Budget and Finance. *United States Department of Agriculture Budget Authority and Outlays, 1971–1973 Budget*, January 1972.

U.S. Department of Health, Education, and Welfare. *Children at the Crossroad, 1970: A Report on State Programs for the Education of Migrant Children Under Title I of the Elementary and Secondary Education Act* (Washington, D.C.: Government Printing Office, 1970).

U.S. Department of Health, Education, and Welfare. Public Health Service. *Ten-State Nutrition Survey in the United States, 1968–1970: Preliminary Report to the Congress, April 1971*, Atlanta, 1971.

U.S. Department of Labor. *Federal Labor Laws and Agencies: A Layman's Guide*, Bulletin No. 123, Revised, Washington, 1957.

U.S. Department of Labor. *A Guide to Child Labor Provisions of the Fair Labor Standards Act*, Child Labor Bulletin No. 101, Revised (Washington, D.C.: Government Printing Office, 1971).

U.S. Department of Labor. *Status of Agricultural Workers Under State and Federal Labor Laws*, Washington, D.C., December 1965.

U.S. Department of Labor. *Working Children: A Report on Child Labor* (5 volumes), Washington, D.C., 1967–1971.

U.S. Office of Economic Opportunity. Migrant Division. *High School Equivalency Program Fact Book,* Washington, D.C., 1971.

U.S. President's Commission on Migratory Labor. *Migratory Labor in American Agriculture,* Report of the President's Commission on Migratory Labor (Washington, D.C.: Government Printing Office, 1951).

State Government Documents

California. Department of Education. *Education for Farm Migrant Children.* Sacramento, 1971.

California. Legislature. Assembly. Committee on Health and Welfare. *Malnutrition: One Key to the Poverty Cycle.* Sacramento, 1970.

California. Department of Industrial Relations. Division of Labor Statistics' and Research. *California Work Injuries, 1969.* San Francisco, 1970.

California. Department of Industrial Relations. Division of Labor Statistics and Research. *Work Injuries in California Agriculture: 1951–1968.* Sacramento (volume for each year).

California. Department of Public Health. *National Nutrition Survey in California.* Berkeley, November 1971.

California. Department of Public Health. Bureau of Maternal and Child Health. Farm Workers Health Service. *Health for the Harvesters: Decade of Hope, 1960–1970: A Ten-Year Report.* December 1970.

Florida. University of Miami. Florida Migratory Child Survey Center. *Migrant Children in Florida: The Phase II Report of the Florida Migratory Child Survey Project, 1968–1969,* by Dr. E. John Kleinert. Miami (n.d.).

Georgia. Department of Education. Migrant Advancement Program. *Migrant Education Newsletter,* Vol. II, No. 1. Atlanta, May 1970.

Michigan. Civil Rights Commission. *A Field Study of Migrant Workers in Michigan.* Detroit, 1969.

New York. Cornell University. College of Agriculture. *Accidents in Agriculture: A Survey of Their Causes and Prevention,* by Paul R. Hoff. Ithaca, 1970.

New York. Department of Education. The University of the State of New York. *Educating Migrant Children.* Albany, 1968.

Ohio. Department of Industrial Relations. *Migratory Labor in Ohio Agriculture*, Sarah R. Dalbey, ed. Columbus, 1968 and 1970.

Oregon. Board of Health. *Oregon Migrant Health Project: 1969 Annual Report*. Portland, 1969.

Oregon. State Employment Service. *Annual Rural Manpower Report, 1970*. Salem (n.d.).

Texas. Southwest Educational Development Laboratory. Texas Educational Development Center. *Evaluation of Migrant Education in Texas: Final Report*. Austin, 1968.

Private Reports

Abuse of Power: Florida Rural Housing Problems and the Farmers Home Administration. American Friends Service Committee, Rural Housing Alliance. Washington, October 1971.

Child Labor in Agriculture, Summer 1970. American Friends Service Committee. Philadelphia, 1971.

Child Labor Among Cotton Growers of Texas, by Charles E. Gibbons. National Child Labor Committee. New York, 1925.

The Condition of Farm Workers and Small Farmers in 1970, by James M. Pierce. National Sharecroppers Fund. New York, 1970.

Day Haul Summer Project, by Margaret DeMarco. American Friends Service Committee. Philadelphia, 1970.

The Excepted People: The Migrant Workers in Washington State, by Tom J. Chambers, Jr. Washington State Council of Churches. Seattle (n.d.).

"Farm Resident Accidents," 1969 and 1970, *Accident Facts*, 1970 and 1971 editions. National Safety Council, Chicago, 1970, 1971.

Hard Tomatoes, Hard Times: The Failure of the Land Grant College Complex, by Jim Hightower. Agribusiness Accountability Project. Washington, 1972.

Is It "More Blessed to Give Than to Receive"?: A Study of Federally Subsidized Grower Attitudes Toward Federal Assistance to the Poor, by Robert L. Gnaizda. California Rural Legal Assistance, Inc. San Francisco (n.d.).

Pieces and Scraps: Farm Labor Housing in the United States, by Lee P. Reno. Rural Housing Alliance. Washington, 1970.

Preliminary Survey and Resource Analysis of South Florida Agribusiness.
Florida Rural Legal Services, Inc. February 1971.
*Resolved, That the Proposed Twentieth Amendment to the Constitution of the
United States Should be Ratified: Debate*, Affirmative, Owen R.
Lovejoy; Negative, Charles S. Thomas. Proceedings of the National
Conference of Social Work for the National Child Labor Committee.
New York, June 1925.

Medical Journals

Chase, H. Peter (M.D.), et al., "Nutritional Status of Preschool Mexican-
American Migrant Farm Children," *American Journal of Diseases of
Children*, Vol. 122, October 1971.
Texas Nutrition Survey Team, "Nutrition Survey in Texas: Preliminary
Findings," *Texas Medicine*, 65:3 (March 1969), pp. 40–49.
Winick, Myron (M.D.), "Biological Correlations," *American Journal of
Diseases of Children*, Vol. 120, November 1970.
Winick, Myron (M.D.), "Cellular Growth During Early Malnutrition," *Pediat-
rics*, 47:6 (June 1971).
Winick, Myron (M.D.), "Changes in Nucleic Acid and Protein Content of
the Human Brain During Growth," *Separatum* Pediat. Res. 2:352–355,
1968.
Winick, Myron (M.D.), "Fetal Malnutrition and Growth Processes," *Hospital
Practice*, May 1970.
Winick, Myron (M.D.), "Food, Time, and Cellular Growth of Brain," *New
York State Journal of Medicine*, 69:2 (January 15, 1969).
Winick, Myron (M.D.), "Nutrition and Mental Development," *Medical
Clinics of North America*, 54:6 (November 1970).
Winick, Myron (M.D.), "Nutrition and Nerve Cell Growth," *Proceedings*
of the American Societies for Experimental Biology, 29:4 (July–August
1970).

Magazines

Ballesteros, David, "Toward an Advantaged Society: Bilingual Education in
the 70's," *The National Elementary Principal*, 50:2 (November 1970).

"Child Labor at the White House Conference," *The American Child*, 22:3 (March 1940).

Drew, Elizabeth, "Going Hungry in America: Government's Failure," *The Atlantic*, December 1968.

Hall, George A., "Court Decision on Agricultural Child Labor," *The American Child*, 21:9 (December 1939).

Rivera, Vidal A., "The Forgotten Ones: Children of Migrants," *The National Elementary Principal*, 50:2 (November 1970).

Wellford, Harrison, "Agribusiness: Overkill on the Farm," *The Washington Monthly*, September 1971.

Index

213